Programming for Linguists

Programming for Linguists:
Perl for Language Researchers

Michael Hammond

Blackwell
Publishing

350 Main Street, Malden, MA 02148–5018, USA
108 Cowley Road, Oxford OX4 1JF, UK
550 Swanston Street, Carlton South, Melbourne, Victoria 3053, Australia
Kurfürstendamm 57, 10707 Berlin, Germany

First published 2003 by Blackwell Publishing Ltd

Library of Congress Cataloging-in-Publication Data

Hammond, Michael (Michael T.)
    Programming for linguistics : Perl for language researchers / Michael Hammond.
        p. cm.
    Includes bibliographical references and index.
    ISBN 0-631-23433-0 (alk. paper) — ISBN 0-631-23434-9 (pbk. : alk. paper)
    1. Computational linguistics.   2. Perl (Computer program language)   I. Title.

P98 .H344 2003
410′.285—dc21

2002034221

A catalogue record for this title is available from the British Library.

Set in 10.5/13pt Sabon
by Graphicraft Limited, Hong Kong
Printed and bound in the United Kingdom
by MPG Books Ltd, Bodmin, Cornwall

For further information on
Blackwell Publishing, visit our website:
http://www.blackwellpublishing.com

Contents

Preface

Computational literacy is essential for the modern linguist or related language professional; for example, speech pathologists, psycholinguists, literary theorists, and so on. Simple programming expertise is an essential part of many forms of data collection and analysis in these fields. Unfortunately, people interested in language often have little or no math background and are sometimes put off by typical programming courses.

This book undertakes to introduce a completely naive person to the rudiments of Perl programming. Through a series of simple examples and exercises, the reader is gradually introduced to the essentials of good programming. The examples are carefully constructed so as to make the introduction of new concepts as simple as possible, while at the same time using sample programs that make sense to someone who works with language as data. Many of these programs can be used immediately, with minimal or no modification.

How is this Book Different?

A number of books on Perl are available. How is this book different from the rest?

First, the most important respect in which this book is different is that it focuses on language. The book is intended for readers interested in using Perl to help them understand language.

Second, unlike many books, every example given is a full program and can stand alone. Thus, for the reader starting from scratch, there is minimal mystery in applying material from any example.

Third, the book is written for a naive reader who may know *nothing* about programming. No prior programming experience is assumed *whatsoever*.

What this Book Isn't

This is not a book on computational linguistics. I spend no time modeling linguistic theory or discussing theory of any sort. Readers who are interested in language but who have no interest in modern linguistic theory should have no fear that knowledge of that field might be required, or that we will be preoccupied with the minutiae of linguistic theory.[1]

This book is not a compendium on Perl. There are many details that are left aside. The goal is to expose the naive reader with an interest in language to the most usable aspects of Perl, those most relevant for writing programs that deal with language.

This is not a Book on Java™

I have written a previous book on the **Java** programming language. Although I have used similar arguments here for why someone interested in language should know how to program, Java and Perl are very different kinds of language. For example, Java offers a rich system for building graphical user interfaces, while generic Perl does not. On the other hand, Perl has built-in support for pattern-matching based on regular expressions, while Java does not. There are a host of other differences as well.

As a consequence, while this book begins with a rather similar structure to the Java book, the structures rapidly depart. While the Java book deals extensively with graphics, this book does not. Moreover, I spend substantially more time in this book on the niceties of regular expressions.

Website

The text is accompanied by exercises at the end of each chapter and all the code is available from the companion website:

http://www.u.arizona.edu/~hammond

Answers to selected even-numbered exercises are also available on the website.

Michael Hammond
July 2002

---

[1] Though how anybody could be left cold by all those minutiae is a mystery to the linguist–author!

Acknowledgments

Thanks to Sean Burke, Rachel Hayes, Will Lewis, Tania Zamuner, and an anonymous reviewer for much useful feedback. Thanks also to my wife Diane, my son Joe, and my constant programming partner Puck. All errors and omissions are my own.

Chapter 1
Why Programming and Why Perl?

This chapter provides two central premises for the rest of the book. First, why would a linguist, psycholinguist, literary theorist, and so on want to know anything about programming? Second, why would Perl be a good choice?

1.1   Why Programming?

Working with language data is nearly impossible these days without a computer. Data are massaged, analyzed, sorted, and distributed on computers. Various software packages are available for language researchers, but to truly take control of this domain, some amount of programming expertise is essential. Consider the following simple examples.

Imagine that you are a syntactician interested in the use of present-tense verbs. You have an electronic corpus and want to find all the cases of verbs in the present tense. How do you do it?

You're a literary stylist and want to investigate the distribution of words with iambic stress in Milton's poetry.

Imagine you are a phonologist. You're interested in consonant clusters. You have an electronic dictionary and want to find the largest word-final consonant cluster. Do you go through it by hand?

Finally, you're a psycholinguist and you want to perform an experiment investigating how people syllabify nonsense words.

All of these are fairly typical research tasks. If you don't know how to program yourself, you have only limited options. One possibility is to do the job by hand. For example, the syntactician could simply print out the corpus and go through it line by line. If the corpus is small enough, this might not be so onerous, but if the corpus is large, or if one really wants to be sure of one's results, then this method is fraught with peril (and really boring). Another solution is to hire somebody else to do the job, but the same considerations apply. Yet a third possibility is to make use of some existing software package.

This last option is occasionally workable, but can fall short in several ways. First, an existing package is restricted by its design. That is, your needs may not match what the software was designed to do, rendering your task impossible or very difficult. Moreover, the software may not be intuitive, and may require learning some arcane set of commands or some difficult control language.[1] Finally, while software may exist to do what you want, it may not be available on the platform you work on (Windows, Mac, Unix), or may be too costly.

1.2   *Why Perl?*

The **Perl** programming language may provide an answer. There are a number of reasons why Perl may be an excellent choice.

First, Perl was designed for extracting information from text files. This makes it ideal for many of the kinds of tasks language researchers need.

Second, there are free Perl implementations for every type of computer. It doesn't matter what kind of operating system you use or computer architecture it's running on. There is a free Perl implementation available.

Third, it's *free*. Again, for any imaginable computer configuration, there is a free Perl implementation.

Fourth, it's extremely easy. In fact, it might not be an exaggeration to claim that of the languages that can do the kinds of things language researchers need, Perl may be the easiest to learn.

Fifth, Perl is an interpreted language. This means that you can write and run your programs immediately without going through an explicit intermediate stage to convert your program into something that the computer will understand.

Sixth, Perl is a natural choice for programming for the web. In chapter 9, I'll show how this presents some very useful opportunities to the language researcher.

Finally, Perl is a powerful programming language. While Perl is optimized for text manipulation, it can be used for just about anything else that one might want to do with a programming language.[2]

What this means is that learning all of Perl would be a monumental task. We won't let this deter us though. My strategy will be to pick and choose. I'll introduce those bits of Perl necessary to do the kinds of things people who work with language typically want to do. The rest – all the bells and whistles we don't need on our train – we'll leave for later. I'll let you know where they are and how to find out more, but we won't digress to deal with them here.

1.3   Download and Install Perl

You may already have Perl on your system. If you're using some flavor of Unix, type perl -v. If you already have Perl, the program should display what version you have. It's possible that you have Perl, but that the program is not in your path. To check if it's anywhere on your system, you can use the where or whereis commands.

Under Windows, you should call up the **MS-DOS** prompt, and again type perl -v. If Perl is on your system, but not in your path, you can use the Windows Find File function to search for perl.exe.

For Macintosh, there is only one implementation of Perl, called **MacPerl**. Find the MacPerl icon and click on it.[3]

If you do not have Perl on your computer system, you can obtain it for free over the web. The following URL provides links to all implementations of Perl: http://www.cpan.org.

At the time of writing, the most recent version of Perl available is version 5. You should make sure that you have access to this version (or later), as the previous version (4) is lacking a number of important properties.

1.4   How to Read this Book

Learning to program isn't really hard, but you do need to do it the right way. The key is to start programming right away. As you read this book, you should make sure to try out the programs as we go through them. In fact, it would be ideal to read the book *at the computer*. Also, don't forget to try the exercises! You'll note that answers are not given at the end of the book. This is for two reasons. First, having answers is a big temptation. More importantly, however, most of the exercises involve revising or writing programs. There are often many ways to achieve the same goal and I would rather you find *some* way to answer an exercise question than feel you have to find *my* way of answering one of them.

Start by running the example programs exactly as given, either by downloading them from the website or, even better, by typing them in yourself. (Typing them in yourself will make the task familiar and draw your attention to aspects of the code you might miss otherwise.)

When you start to feel more comfortable, try varying the code a bit. The programs up through chapter 3 are perfectly safe and variations can't harm your computer. After that point, certain operations should be handled with care, but I'll warn you about those as we go through.

The key, though, is to have fun!

Notes

[1] This latter point may seem analogous to learning a programming language, but notice that learning an arcane set of commands doesn't generalize; you would need to do that for every separate package that you have.

[2] The only place where Perl is lacking is in terms of graphics and graphical user interfaces. It's not possible to directly construct windows, buttons, and the like all in Perl. There are very reasonable ways around this limit, however. For example, as I discuss in appendix B, the optional Tk module allows for graphical user interfaces and other graphical programming.

[3] As of MacOS X, generic Unix Perl is available for Macs as well.

Chapter 2

Getting Started

This chapter explains how Perl works and introduces the edit–run cycle for readers with no background in programming. I begin with how to edit a file using any number of editors, and go on to explain how to compile and run the programs we write.

2.1   Edit and Run

Just in case you've never written a computer program in your life, let's go over the basic idea. A programming language allows you to issue instructions to your computer. In effect, it is a lingua franca, a mediating language. You translate your ideas into it and the computer translates it into something it can understand: **machine code**.

The process of writing up your program in the programming language is the **edit** phase. Once you've written out your program in Perl, you then convert it to machine code and run it using the perl command. This is referred to as the **run** phase. Let's go through each of these in turn.

2.1.1   Edit

You need to create your program using some sort of text editor. In principle, you can use any editor, but it's easiest to use a very simple one. There are a number of possibilities and I list some of them below. The key component is that the file you create should be saved as a **text** file with the extension ".pl". This can certainly be done with a normal text editor, but is often easier to do with one of these:

Windows   Edit, Notepad, Vim, TextPad, and so on.
Mac   MacPerl, SimpleText, Alpha, BBEdit, and so on.
Unix   Emacs, Vi(m), Pico, and so on.

Let's go through how to create a program using the **MS-DOS** command edit under Windows. First, open the MS-DOS prompt on the program menu of Windows. Switch to an appropriate directory using the cd command. For example, if you plan to put all your Perl programs in an existing directory myperl, you would switch to that directory using the command cd \myperl.

Once you're in the appropriate directory, it's time to edit a program file. To create a Perl program file called helloworld.pl, type the following in the DOS window: edit helloworld.pl. This will bring up a simple text editor into which we will type our code. Type the following into the window *exactly*:

```
print("Hello World!");
```

To save your code, select save from the File menu. Then choose quit from the same menu to exit back to the DOS window.

Let's go through the code that you typed in very briefly. I'll treat it in more depth later on, but let's just get a sense of what you just did. First, programs have two basic organizational units: **statements** and **groups**. Statements are instructions for the computer to carry out. They are always terminated by a semicolon and are executed in sequence from top to bottom. Groups indicate the organization of statements into larger units and are always marked with curly braces.[1] In this particularly simple example, there is only a single statement and no groups.

The single statement here is the print() command applied to the string "Hello World!". There are many more details and nuances to even this little snippet of code, but I'll defer these to later.

2.1.2   Run

The next step is to translate your program into something that your computer will understand and run. You do this by typing the following at the command line:

```
perl helloworld.pl
```

The computer should whir away for a second or two and then print out this string: Hello World!.

If something has gone wrong, then you will get a perhaps cryptic error message. There are really only three possibilities. One is that you did not actually create the helloworld.pl file or did not save it in the right form. To check this under Windows, type type helloworld.pl. The file should scroll by in a legible form.

If that worked, and perl helloworld.pl still doesn't work, then you must have made some sort of error in typing in the original program. Open the file again with your text editor and confirm that it is exactly as above.

A third possibility under Windows or Unix is that perl is not in your path. Follow the instructions appropriate to your operating system to correct this. For Windows, this typically involves editing the autoexec.bat file. For Unix, this typically involves making changes to your .login file or your .cshrc file (or its equivalent). These are delicate tasks though, so you should seek assistance before attempting them on your own if you've never done this before.

2.2   Other Platforms

Running Perl programs under Unix is essentially the same as under Windows. There are different editors, and the command prompt is always available, but the steps are essentially the same.

For Macintosh, it goes a little differently. Assuming the MacPerl implementation of Perl, there are two differences. First, there is no command-line prompt on a Mac. Second, the editor is integrated into the MacPerl program. To do the same example as above, double-click on the MacPerl icon to bring up the editor. Edit the program exactly as above. Save it as helloworld.pl, using the Save command from the File menu. Then choose Run from the MacPerl menu.

2.3   Summary

This chapter has introduced the basic task of writing and running programs. We went through a very simple example, but the procedure will remain the same for programs of any complexity.

2.4   Exercises

1.   Change the text that's printed when helloworld.pl is run.
2.   Alter the helloworld.pl program so that it prints two different things.
3.   Take the helloworld.pl program, rename it, and run it again.

Note

[1] I treat groups in the next chapter.

Chapter 3

Basics: Control Structures and Variables

In this chapter, I cover the basic structures of Perl. I start with the idea of a computer program as a sequence of commands. I then introduce different data types and different types of variables to hold these data types. The body of the chapter is taken up with a discussion of the basic control structures.

The chapter concludes with a demonstration of how even this little snippet of Perl can be used to solve problems of linguistic interest, here the construction of materials for psycholinguistic experiments.

3.1   Statements

Programs in Perl are composed of a sequence of commands. Each command typically appears on a separate line terminated with a semicolon. For example, the helloworld.pl program in the preceding chapter was composed of a single command. Here is a more complex program composed of two commands:[1]

`hello2.pl`

```
print("Hello");
print("there!");
```

This program first prints out the word Hello, and then prints out the string there!. This produces an interaction like the following:

```
> perl hello2.pl
Hello there! >
```

Notice how the prompt appears on the same line as the string that Perl printed. Notice too how the two different print() commands ended up on the same line. We can remedy this by adding in an explicit return – or newline – character in the string printed: \n. The above program is revised below:

hello3.pl

```
print("Hello\n");
print("there!\n");
```

Typed at the prompt, this program produces this interaction:

```
> perl hello3.pl
Hello
there!
>
```

So far, having two separate statements doesn't do any more work than having a single statement. This is only an artifact of the fact that so far we have only a single command print(). The following program does the same work as the preceding one, but with only a single statement:

hello4.pl

```
print("Hello\nthere!\n");
```

Before going on to add additional commands to our repertoire, we need to treat primitive data types.

3.2 *Numbers and Strings*

For our purposes, there are really only two data types that we need to concern ourselves with: numbers and strings. Perl can manipulate numbers just like strings. For example, numbers can be printed:

numprint1.pl

```
print(3);
```

Numbers can also be manipulated by the usual numerical operations; for example, +, −, *, /, %, and so on.[2] The following program shows how these can be used with the print() command:

`numprint2.pl`

```
print 3 + 4;
print(" ");
print(5 * 2);
print(" ");
print(3 - 9);
print(" ");
print(9 / 3);
print(" ");
print(10 % 3);
print("\n");
```

All other mathematical operators are available as well. (Incidentally, if it isn't apparent, the command print(" "); prints a single space.)

Strings are somewhat different than numbers and must always be quoted: for example, "hat" or 'hat'. The difference between single and double quotes is that special characters are not available in single-quoted strings. For example, \n is not interpreted as return if it appears in a single-quoted string. Either kind of quote is adequate for the print() command, as exemplified in the following program:

`stringprint.pl`

```
print("hat\n");
print('chair\n');
```

This program produces the following interaction at the prompt:

```
> perl stringprint.pl
hat
chair\n >
```

Only the first \n is interpreted as a return since the second \n is enclosed in single quotes. We will see in the next section that there are additional differences between single and double quotes.

There are various operations that can be performed with strings as well. One of the most useful is concatenation. The operator for this is period (full stop). The following little program shows how this works:

`stringconcat.pl`

```
print("string" . " " . "concatenation\n");
```

This program concatenates three strings and prints out the string string concatenation.

3.3 *Variables*

Variables allow one to store information for later use.[3] For example, one can assign the result of some mathematical operation to a variable and then use the print() command to print out the contents of the variable later. This turns out to be an essential aspect of any sort of programming.

Variables are extremely easy to define and use in Perl. First, a variable is simply any string of letters, numbers, or underlines (where the first character must be a letter or underline) preceded by the special character $. For example, the following are all legal variable names: $i, $_i, $variable, $i47, $my_vbl, $myVbl.

The following program shows how this works:

varex1.pl

```
$myvariable = 4 + 2;
print("The variable is: ");
print($myvariable);
print("\n");
```

First, the variable $myvariable is assigned the result of adding 4 and 2. A string is printed, then the contents of the variable, and then the return is printed.

Variables can also be used in mathematical operations. For example, the following program shows how numbers can be assigned to variables and then mathematical operations performed on those variables:

varex2.pl

```
$one = 2;
$two = 3;
$three = $one + $two;
print($three);
print("\n");
```

The program uses some particularly confusing variable names so as to dramatize the difference between the *name* of a variable and the *contents* of that variable. Here the variable $one is assigned the contents or value 2; the variable $two is assigned the value 3. The contents of $one and $two are added together, which produces 5 (not 3!). The result of that operation is put in another variable called $three, which is then printed out. The reader should make very sure to understand why this program prints out 5 and not some other value.

Strings can also be put into variables as well, as exemplified in the following program:

varex3.pl

```
$hat = "chair";
$chair = "hat";
print($hat);
print("\n");
print($chair);
print("\n");
```

Again, I've used particularly inappropriate variable names to make clear that the name of the variable is not to be confused with its value. For example, in the above program, the variable $chair does not have the value chair, but the value or contents hat.

Variables can also be used in strings. For example, the above program can be simplified by enclosing all the variables in double quotes as follows:

varex4.pl

```
$hat = "chair";
$chair = "hat";
print("$hat\n$chair\n");
```

This produces exactly the same output as the preceding program.

Finally, note that variables in singly-quoted strings are not interpreted, but are treated as literal strings. Thus if we assign the value of 3 to a variable $hat, and try to print "$hat", we will get 3. On the other hand, if we try to print '$hat', we will get literally $hat. The following program shows how this works:

varex5.pl

```
$hat = 3;
print("$hat\n");
print('$hat\n');
```

This produces output as follows:

```
> perl varex5.pl
3
$hat\n>
```

Variables are not much use until we have some way of collecting information from outside. The most useful way to do this is either from a file or from the user, but there are other ways as well. As a rather silly example (though one that makes use of some commands that will be useful later), consider the following program. It makes use of two new commands. The first, time(), returns the total number of seconds since January 1, 1970. The second new command is getlogin(), which returns the name of the current user.[4] The program below first collects the start time and stores it in a variable $start. Next, the program collects the user's login name and stores it in a variable $name. It then prints out a personalized greeting based on the value of $name. It then collects a second end time and stores that in a variable $end. It computes the difference between the two times and stores that in $diff, and then prints it out.

varex6.pl

```
$start = time();
$name = getlogin();
print("Hello, $name!\n");
$end = time();
$diff = $end - $start;
print("That took $diff seconds.\n");
```

On most systems, the time to accomplish such a trivial task should be negligible, producing a difference of less than a second, which when evaluated in this fashion should come out to 0. You might trying adding additional statements in between the relevant statements above to force the computer to take longer. This is a useful exercise to get a sense of how long it takes your computer to do things. Although the time taken for this task is negligible, we will soon see that it's possible to write programs that take quite a bit of time to run.

3.4   Arrays

Another extremely useful data structure is an **array**. Arrays are really just sequences of variables that are grouped together. They are a convenient way of keeping track of a list of items. For example, one might store a list of verbs in an array called @verbs. Array names are subject to the same alphanumeric requirements as variable names. One key difference is that the array name is preceded by the special character @, rather than $.

Individual array elements (the individual items in the sequence grouped together by the array) are referred to by indices, where the index numbers begin with zero! In addition, individual array elements are prefixed by $, rather than @.[5] Thus the entire array containing the list of verbs might be called @verbs, but the individual elements of that array will be called $verbs[0], $verbs[1], $verbs[2], and so on. Here's a very simple program showing how these can be used:

arr1.pl

```
$verb[0] = "run";
$verb[1] = "jump";
$verb[2] = "sing";
print("The three verbs are: $verb[0], $verb[1], and $verb[2].\n");
```

So far, arrays aren't much good, except for the conceptual advantage of having similar names for variables that contain similar content. However, arrays can be assigned and recovered simultaneously as well. The following program performs almost exactly the same way as the preceding program, except that the array is assigned in one fell swoop and retrieved in the same way:

arr2.pl

```
@verb = ("run", "jump", "sing");
print("The three verbs are: @verb.\n");
```

Parentheses are used to demarcate a **list** of items. Since the entire array is being assigned to, we use @verb, rather than $verb[0], and so on.

The only difference in how the programs work is how the @verb is interpreted in the print() command:

```
first one: The three verbs are: run, jump, and sing.
second one: The three verbs are: run jump sing.
```

In the latter case, the individual elements of the array in double quotes are printed with only a space as a separator.

Arrays are actually an incredibly useful device. This is only apparent when we consider how they can be used with the various control structures Perl provides. I cover this in the next section.

3.5 Control Structures

The **control structures** of a programming language are powerful tools. These allow you to group together commands into larger units and impose dependencies between the results of one command and other commands. In addition, these structures allow you to iterate in various ways. These are essential for programming tasks of any complexity.

Perl provides all of the usual control structures and a few more to boot. I go through these in the next few sections.[6]

3.5.1 if

The most common and most useful control structure is the if structure. This allows a statement or **block** of statements to be executed only if some condition is true. The usual form of an if structure is for the keyword if to come first, followed by the conditional clause in parentheses, followed by any number of statements – a **block** – surrounded by curly braces:

if (condition) { any number of statements }

For example, the following program prints out the results of a particular equation only if two plus two is actually greater than three (which is, of course, always true):

ifex1.pl

```
if (2 + 2 > 3) {
    print("The laws of math still hold!");
}
```

In fact, any number of statements can occur within the curly braces. For example:

ifex2.pl

```
if (2 + 2 < 5) {
    $result = 2 + 2;
    print("The result is $result.\n");
}
```

The if-clause can contain any number of logical tests. Here are some of the most useful ones:

Numerical	String	Meaning
>	gt	Greater than
<	lt	Less than
>=	ge	Greater than or equal
<=	le	Less than or equal
==	eq	Equal
!=	ne	Not equal

These can also be combined using the logical connectives and or or.[7]

We've already seen examples of some of the numerical comparisons, but not the equality comparison. Notice that the symbol to test for whether two numerical expressions are equal is ==, *not* =. This is an extremely common error. Consider the following example:

ifex3.pl

```
$number = 4;
if ($number == 2 + 2) {
    print("$number\n");
}
```

This will print out the contents of the variable $number just in case it has a value of 4. The following program prints nothing, as the numerical test fails:

ifex4.pl

```
$number = 4;
if ($number == 2 + 3) {
    print("$number\n");
}
```

Now consider what happens if we *incorrectly* replace the numerical equality test == with the assignment operator =:

ifex5.pl

```
$number = 4;
if ($number = 2 + 3) {
    print("$number\n");
}
```

Not only does the if-clause return true here, but the value printed is 5, not 4. This is because using the assignment operator = in the if-clause reassigns the value of $number to 5. In addition, since that reassignment succeeds, the if-clause is evaluated as true. Hence, when the print() clause is executed, it prints the new value of $number. Again, this is an *extremely* common mistake and you should be careful to avoid it.

Finally, let's look at some numerical comparisons using the logical connectives and and or. Here is a numerical example of or:

ifex6.pl

```
$x = 4;
$y = -7;
if ($x < 17 or $y == 6) {
   print("$x and $y\n");
}
```

The program tests whether $x is less than 17 or $y equals 6. If either condition holds, their values are printed out. Replacing or with and would result in nothing being printed. Both conditions would have to hold for the if-clause to be true.

Let's now consider the string comparison operators. The first thing to notice is that they are different. For example, comparing any two strings with == will always return true, while eq only returns true if the strings are identical. The comparison operators for strings allow one to compare strings for alphabetic order. The following program exemplifies:

ifex7.pl

```
if ("hats" eq "hat" . "s") {
   print("yes\n");
}
if ("had" lt "hat") {
   print("yes again\n");
}
```

String and numerical comparisons can of course be combined with the logical connectives:

ifex8.pl

```
$word = "chair";
$number = 7;
if ($word gt "chair" and $number <= 7) {
   print("Yippee!\n");
}
```

This program assigns the string "chair" to $word, and the number 7 to the variable $number. The if-clause tests if the value of $word (which is "chair") is alphabetically before the string "chair" and whether the contents of $number are less than or equal to 7. Since only the latter is true, the if-clause is false and nothing is printed.

The if structure has several variants. One of the most useful is else. The block of statements that apply when the if-clause is true can optionally be followed by another block of statements that apply if the if-clause is *not* true:

if (condition) { any number of statements } else { more statements }

This can be quite useful:

ifex9.pl

```
$furniture = "chairs";
$headgear = "hats";
if ($furniture lt $headgear) {
    print("Put $furniture first.\n");
} else {
    print("Put $headgear first.\n");
}
```

Here, the program prints out an appropriate message indicating which string is alphabetically prior to the other.

The if structure also allows for optional elsif clauses, with or without a final else-clause:

if (condition) { any number of statements } elsif (condition) { more statements }

For example, the following little program shows how an elsif can be used:

ifex10.pl

```
$result = (60/3) * 1.5;
if ($result > 100) {
    print("Too big.\n");
} elsif ($result < 2) {
    print("Too small.\n");
} else {
    print("Just right: $result.\n");
}
```

In fact, there can be any number of elsifs after the initial if, with or without a final else. The following program exemplifies:

ifex11.pl

```
$result = 6 * .5;
if ($result == 1) {
    print("1\n");
} elsif ($result * 3 == 6) {
    print("something small\n");
} elsif ($result == 0) {
    print("nothing\n");
}
```

This program actually produces no output.

If-structures can also be embedded:

ifex12.pl

```
$name = getlogin();
print("Your name is: $name\n");
if ($name lt 'b') {
    print("Your name begins with 'a'.\n");
    if ($name lt 'ab') {
        print("Your name must be 'aardvark'!\n");
    }
}
```

This program tests whether the user's login name begins with an "a". If it does, the program then tests whether it begins with an "aa".

Finally, just in case the consequent is a single statement, there is an alternative abbreviated form of the if-structure. The ifex7.pl program on page 17 can also be written as follows:

ifex13.pl

```
print("yes\n") if ("hats" eq "hat" . "s");
print("yes again\n") if ("had" lt "hat");
```

3.5.2   while

Another extremely useful structure is the while-loop:

while (while-condition) { any number of statements }

The while-loop allows a set of statements to be repeated as long as some condition is true. The following example shows how the while-structure can be used to iterate a command a specified number of times:

whileex1.pl

```
$i = 0;
while ($i < 10) {
    print("$i\n");
    $i = $i + 1;
}
```

First, the variable $i is initialized to 0. The while-condition tests whether $i is less than 10. Since it is, the block of statements is evaluated. First, the value of $i is printed out, and then the value of $i is augmented by one.

Pay careful attention to the logic of the while-structure. You must always be careful to provide a mechanism to end the iteration. For example, here the value of the variable $i is checked at each iteration for whether it exceeds the threshold of 10. We include in the body of the while-structure a statement that guarantees that with each iteration, $i will get closer to that threshold.

If you do not provide an exit condition, or do so incorrectly, you run the risk of your program iterating forever – or until the user gets bored and stops the program with ctrl-c (cmd-. for Mac users).

The above program uses an explicit counter to control the while-condition. This is so very common that Perl has simplified syntax to increment or decrement a variable; that is, $i++ and $i--. The above program can be rewritten as follows:

whileex2.pl

```
$i = 0;
while ($i < 10) {
    print("$i\n");
    $i++;
}
```

As you may have guessed, the whole program can be rewritten using a decremented variable instead:

whileex3.pl

```
$i = 10;
while ($i > 0) {
    print("$i\n");
    $i--;
}
```

This program prints the integers out in the opposite order.

The while-structure does not need to refer to an explicitly incremented or decremented counter. The following program shows how a while-structure can be used to wait a specified amount of time, here 5 seconds:

whileex4.pl

```
$then = time();
$diff = 0;
while ($diff < 6) {
    $now = time();
    $diff = $now - $then;
}
print("done!\n");
```

The program first collects the current time and stores it in a variable $then. It then initializes a variable $diff to 0. The $diff variable will be used to store the elapsed time. The program next enters a while-structure which iterates until $diff exceeds 5. The statements in the while-structure collect the current time and then calculate the elapsed time, storing it in $diff. When the elapsed time reaches 6, the while-structure is exited and a final message is printed.

There is an alternate form of the while-structure where the while-condition is checked *after* the statements are executed:

do { any number of statements } while (while-condition);

If the while-condition is true, the statement block iterates again. Using the do/while-structure, the above program can be rewritten as follows:

whileex5.pl

```
$then = time();
do {
    $now = time();
    $diff = $now - $then;
} while ($diff < 6);
print("done!\n");
```

There are two things to notice about the do/while-structure. First, notice that it must be terminated with a semicolon, unlike the simple while-structure. Second, the do/while-structure can result in slightly different behavior, given when the while-condition is checked. Compare the output of the program below with that of whileex2.pl on page 20:

whileex6.pl

```
$i = 0;
do {
    print("$i\n");
    $i++;
} while ($i < 10);
```

Both programs produce the same output. However, when the initialization statements are changed from 0 to 10, different outputs result:

whileex7.pl

```
$i = 10;
while ($i < 10) {
    print("$i\n");
    $i++;
}
```

whileex8.pl

```
$i = 10;
do {
    print("$i\n");
    $i++;
} while ($i < 10);
```

The first program prints nothing, as $i already equals 10 when the while-condition is checked. The second program completes one iteration *before* the while-condition is checked, printing out the number 10.

Of course, a while-structure can also be used with an if-structure. Here is an example where a while-structure is embedded in an if/else-structure to calculate factorials; for example, $5! = 5 \cdot 4 \cdot 3 \cdot 2 \cdot 1$. The nested structures are used to capture the perhaps surprising fact that $0! = 1$:

whileex9.pl

```
$num = 5;
if ($num == 0) {
    print("1\n");
} else {
    $res = 1;
    $i = 1;
```

```
    while ($i <= $num) {
        $res = $res * $i;
        $i++;
    }
    print("$res\n");
}
```

3.5.3   for

Counters are so prevalent as a way to control iteration that Perl, like most other programming languages, includes a special structure that keeps track of the counter – the for-structure:

for (counter; limit; increment) { any number of statements }

The for-clause includes three slots, separated by semicolons. The first provides for the initialization of the counter. The second describes the limit of the counter. The third describes how it is incremented (or decremented). With a for-structure, programs like whileex2.pl on page 20 can be rewritten as follows:

forex1.pl

```
for ($i = 0; $i < 10; $i++) {
    print("$i\n");
}
```

The for-structure is actually unnecessary, but it is quite useful nonetheless. It helps you avoid programming mistakes with iteration controlled by a counter, because it forces you to specify all the essential properties of the counter at the outset.[8]

3.5.4   foreach

One of the most useful control structures is the foreach structure:

foreach $vbl (list or array) { any number of statements }

The reserved word foreach is followed by some variable name. This variable takes as its values each of the values provided by the following list or array. The statements in the block can then apply to each value of the list or array using the given variable name. For example, the following program prints out a list of verbs:

foreachex1.pl

```
@verbs = ('run', 'jump', 'hit');
foreach $verb (@verbs) {
    print("$verb\n");
}
```

In fact, the list can be referred to directly in the foreach-structure:

foreachex2.pl

```
foreach $verb ('run', 'jump', 'hit') {
    print("$verb\n");
}
```

If a list is composed of ascending contiguous naturally ordered elements like integers or letters, it can be abbreviated with ..; for example, (1, 2, 3, 4, 5) can be written as (1..5). The following program uses this device to print the numbers 1 through 10:

foreachex3.pl

```
foreach $n (1..10) {
    print("$n\n");
}
```

The following program does the same thing for the first 10 letters of the alphabet:

foreachex4.pl

```
foreach $a ('a'..'j') {
    print("$a\n");
}
```

3.6   *Experimental Materials*

The variables and control structures that we've covered so far are extremely powerful programming tools, but it's difficult to really see this until we cover the various ways to supply data to our programs. However, even at this stage, we can use the devices we've learned about so far to take care of important tasks. In this section, I consider two examples.

Imagine you want to conduct an experiment involving nonsense strings. You have some particular experimental task and you need every possible combination of consonants (Cs) and vowels (Vs) in this pattern: CVCV. It would be a hugely tedious task to generate all of these by hand, but it is a trivial task given what we've learned so far.

Let's consider the problem from a logical perspective. First, we need to define what we mean by consonant and vowel, since Perl does not have such a distinction built in. Second, we need to make sure that for each choice of consonant or vowel, for each position, we create a string of all four segments.

Turning to more concrete steps, we can define two arrays, one for consonants and one for vowels. Membership of one of these arrays constitutes defining a segment as either a consonant or vowel. Combining all possible combinations can be done with four foreach structures, each nested in the previous one.

Let's develop these ideas incrementally. The following program defines the set of consonants as @consonant and the set of vowels as @vowel. It then prints out all the consonants *and then* all the vowels:

expmat1.pl

```
@consonant = ('b','c','d','f','g','h','j','k','l','m',
    'n','p','q','r','s','t','v','w','x','y','z');
@vowel = ('a','e','i','o','u');

foreach $c (@consonant) {
   print("$c\n");
}
foreach $v (@vowel) {
   print("$v\n");
}
```

To combine these so that every vowel is paired with every consonant, we need to nest the foreach loops as follows:

expmat2.pl

```
@consonant = ('b','c','d','f','g','h','j','k','l','m',
    'n','p','q','r','s','t','v','w','x','y','z');
@vowel = ('a','e','i','o','u');

foreach $c (@consonant) {
   foreach $v (@vowel) {
      print("$c$v\n");
   }
}
```

Each time a consonant is selected by the outer loop, a new vowel is selected and both are printed. The next consonant is selected and the process is repeated. Creating all possible CVCV shapes then involves nesting *four* foreach-structures. The following program exemplifies this:

expmat3.pl

```
@consonant = ('b','c','d','f','g','h','j','k','l','m',
    'n','p','q','r','s','t','v','w','x','y','z');
@vowel = ('a','e','i','o','u');

foreach $c1 (@consonant) {
   foreach $v1 (@vowel) {
      foreach $c2 (@consonant) {
         foreach $v2 (@vowel) {
            print("$c1$v1$c2$v2\n");
         }
      }
   }
}
```

This program will print out the 11025 (= 21 · 5 · 21 · 5) different possibilities. Each time a selection is made by one of the foreach loops, the next inner loop iterates through all its choices. So, for example, when $c1 is set to "m", $v1 will iterate through all the vowel possibilities, and so on and so on and so on.[9]

The same sort of thing can of course be done with words and sentences, and this is left as an exercise.

As a second example, consider the problem of determining the prime numbers.[10] Imagine that we wish to know the prime numbers between 1 and some upper bound, say 100.

Thinking about this logically, we need to go through the numbers one by one. For each number, we need to check whether it is divisible by something between 1 and itself. If it is so divisible, then it is not prime. Here is a program that does this:

primes.pl

```
$max = 100;
for ($i = 2; $i <= $max; $i++) {
   $isprime = 0;
   for ($j = 2; $j < $i and $isprime != 1; $j++) {
      $isprime = 1 if ($i % $j == 0);
   }
   print("$i\n") if ($isprime == 0);
}
```

The program makes use of a nested for-structure. The outer for iterates over the integers between 2 and the defined maximum $max. The inner for iterates over all the integers smaller than the current one ($i). For each integer it checks, the program sets the value of a variable $isprime to 0 (or false). If the current number is divisible by something other than itself or one, the value of $isprime is set to 1 (or true). This is done using the modulus operator %, which returns the remainder of a division operation. The $isprime variable is used in two places. First, it is used to control the iteration of the internal for loop. For the iteration to continue, the value of $j must be below $i and the value of $isprime must be 0 (that is, false). Once the inner iteration ends, the value of $isprime is inspected to see if the current value of $i is prime.

The preceding example was rather nonlinguistic, but similar techniques can be required for linguistic purposes. Imagine that we have more specific restrictions on the experimental materials we need in the example preceding; that is, the vowels must be identical, but the consonants must be different. Thus we would be interested in forms such as *poko* and *kopo*, but not *popo* or *poku*. This can be done by making two changes to our earlier program. First, we only use three nested foreach loops, as the vowels are the same. Second, we add an if-structure to test if the two consonants are identical. If they are not, the form is printed:

expmat4.pl

```
@consonant = ('b','c','d','f','g','h','j','k','l','m',
   'n','p','q','r','s','t','v','w','x','y','z');
@vowel = ('a','e','i','o','u');

foreach $c1 (@consonant) {
   foreach $v (@vowel) {
      foreach $c2 (@consonant) {
         print("$c1$v$c2$v\n") if ($c1 ne $c2);
      }
   }
}
```

This is simpler than expmat3.pl in that it has only three foreach loops. It is more complex, however, in that like the primes.pl program, it tests for some condition before printing.

3.7 *Summary*

This chapter has treated the syntactic heart of the Perl language: control structures and variables.

Variables and arrays allow you to store data for later manipulation. Perl is quite convenient on this score for several reasons. First, variables and arrays are all marked with preceding special characters. Hence, in any bit of code, you can always identify what the variables and arrays are. Second, variables can just be invoked wherever you need them (unlike in other programming languages where variables must be *declared* in advance). Finally, variables and arrays are all of one type; there is no difference between variables and arrays that hold strings, or characters, or numbers.

This chapter has also treated the principal control structures of Perl. These are the essence of any program. They allow one to supercede the normal top-down flow of control, allowing for looping, branching, and conditional application of various sorts.

3.8   Exercises

1. Write a program that makes crucial use of *all* of the control structures we've covered in this chapter (if, while, for, and foreach).
2. Write a program that will generate every noun–verb–noun sentence where the nouns are *John, Mary*, and *Joe*, and the verbs are *sees, meets*, and *greets*.
3. Revise the second program above to include *people* and *linguists* as nouns and *see, meet*, and *greet* as verbs. Make sure your program handles number agreement with the subject; for example, *people see*, but *Mary sees*.
4. The primes.pl program is extremely inefficient. Add code so that you can keep track of how long it takes for the program to compute primes in different ranges. (The numbers you get may not be very useful if you are working on a machine that is swapping jobs, such as a large multi-user system.)

Notes

[1] In this and following examples, I give the name of the program in parentheses before the code. This is *not* part of the program and should not go in the program file. This is intended as a convenience to identify programs on the website.

[2] If you're not familiar with it, % is the **modulus** operator; it returns the remainder of dividing the first of its operands by the second.

[3] What I am calling a variable here is called a **scalar** in the technical Perl literature. I use the more intuitive term here.

[4] The getlogin() command behaves as expected under Unix, but may produce differing results under different operating systems. For example, it doesn't work at all under Windows.

[5] It is an extremely common error to mix these up. Be careful!

[6] The only common control structure that is missing in Perl is the switch structure of C. However, this is readily paraphrased with if/elsif.

[7] Perl also includes "high precedence" versions of these as well: && (and) and || (or). "Precedence" controls how expressions with multiple operators and no parentheses are interpreted.

[8] There are a number of other control structures that Perl provides that are also redundant; for example, until, unless, and ?:. Unlike for, these do not have virtues that offset the memory burden of learning them for our purposes, and so I leave them aside.

[9] Under DOS or Unix, the output of this program can be sent to a file with the redirection operator on the command line; for example, perl expmat1.pl > results.txt. File output is treated more generally in chapter 4.

[10] A prime number is a number divisible only by itself and 1; for example, 1, 2, 3, 5, 7, 11, and so on.

Chapter 4

Input and Output

The programs we have written so far have been of limited utility because we haven't really had sufficient options to get data into our programs. In this chapter, I present the principal methods for reading and writing data: **input** and **output** (IO).

4.1 Overview

There are really only two ways to get data into your programs. One is to type it in, and the other is to read it in from some existing file. You can type the data in right when you start your program; this is called **command-line input**. This is appropriate if not much data is required or if the data are needed before the program begins to run. For example, if you had a program printword.pl that printed out a single word, say *apple*, you might enter that word on the command line; for example, perl printword.pl apple.

The other kind of typed input is **prompted input**. In this case, the user enters data while the program is running. This is appropriate in several circumstances. First, the amount of data should be relatively small. Second, this is appropriate if the precise data aren't known until the program has been running. Finally, this is appropriate if the person who starts the program isn't necessarily the person who will be interacting with it.

The other kind of input is file input, where data is read in from a **file**. This is always a preferred method, since it saves the user the effort of typing the data. Huge amounts of data can be read in in this way, so typing the data in by hand may be a virtually impossible alternative.

The computer can return data in several ways: to the screen or to a file. Output to the screen is appropriate where there isn't very much output, or where the output is critical to some prompted input the user might subsequently provide. File output is appropriate where there is a lot of output and where the user is likely to want to keep a record of the output.

Under Unix or Windows/DOS, the distinction may seem a minor one. After all, screen output can always be redirected to a file; for example, perl myprog.pl > myfile.txt. This would print the output of myprog.pl into a file myfile.txt. There are several reasons to reject this as a general solution. First, this option is not available on a Mac.[1] Second, this does not allow us to write different bits of data to different files.

To summarize, the principal IO choices are given in the following table:

	Input	Output
Command line	✓	
Prompt	✓	✓
File	✓	✓

We've actually already treated output to the prompt; this is what the print() command does.[2] In the remainder of this chapter, I'll introduce all the others. As usual, IO is a huge topic, but we will keep to only those aspects likely to be of use to the language researcher.

4.2   The Command Line

Command-line input is quite easy in Perl. Any number of arguments can be entered on the command line after the name of your program. For example, to enter the number 10 as a command-line argument to a program myprog.pl, you would type perl myprog.pl 10.

When your program begins, all its command-line arguments are automatically available in an array called @ARGV. The first command-line argument is $ARGV[0], the second $ARGV[1], and so on. As an example, the following program simply prints out its first command-line argument:

cmdln1.pl

```
print("$ARGV[0]\n");
```

We can also accommodate the situation in which any number of command-line arguments may be entered. Defining any array, say @myarray, automatically defines a variable $#myarray that keeps track of the last index of the corresponding array. For example, if we were to create an array @thearray and put three integers in it, then the variable $#thearray would have the value 2.[3] If the array has no elements in it, then the associated variable has the value −1. Using this general notion, the following program prints out all its command-line arguments:

cmdln2.pl

```
if ($#ARGV == -1) {
   print("No command-line arguments!\n");
} else {
   for ($j = 0; $j <= $#ARGV; $j++) {
      print("$ARGV[$j]\n");
   }
}
```

Here's a similar program that prints out the sum of its command-line arguments:

cmdln3.pl

```
$total = 0;
for ($i = 0; $i <= $#ARGV; $i++) {
   $total = $total + $ARGV[$i];
}
print("Total: $total\n");
```

4.3   *Prompt Input*

Prompt input requires several things: **handles, reading,** and **chomp**ing. For files and prompt input and output, Perl makes use of **handles**. A handle is a name for a particular input or output path. Perl predefines a certain number of these, but new ones can also be defined by the programmer.

Perl predefines the three standard IO paths: standard input, standard output, and standard error. The handle for standard input is STDIN.[4] STDIN is where Perl reads input from. (I'll show below how to do this.) If you want to collect prompt input at some point in your program, you will issue a command for Perl to read from STDIN at that point.

I return to standard output and standard error below. Let's now consider how to read from a handle. Putting the handle in angled brackets reads one record from a handle. A record is predefined as a line.[5] Thus <STDIN> reads a line from the prompt. The following program shows how this can be used to set the value of a variable:

promptex1.pl

```
print("Enter a number: ");
$num = <STDIN>;
print("You entered $num");
```

The program prints an instruction to the user to enter a number. The user then enters a number followed by a return. The program prints back the number with a brief message, producing interchanges such as the following:

```
> perl promptex1.pl
Enter a number: 10
You entered 10
>
```

You'll note that no return was required at the end of the message printed. The <STDIN> command reads in the number and the terminating return and, in this case, assigns it to $num. While this turned out to be convenient for printing the variable in the case at hand, this return would make it impossible to do math, for example, on the number entered. To eliminate the return, we can use the chomp() command:

promptex2.pl

```
print("Enter a number: ");
$num = <STDIN>;
chomp($num);
print("You entered $num\n");
```

The chomp() command removes a string-final return.[6] Now, of course, we must put an explicit return in the final print() statement. Otherwise, the subsequent cursor would appear on the same line.

Here's a second example of prompt input. This program takes a series of lines typed at the prompt, saves them to an array, and then prints them all back at the prompt, along with line numbers:

promptex3.pl

```
$i = 0;
print("Enter text below and a blank line to end.\n");
while ((length($line = <STDIN>)) > 1) {
    $lines[$i++] = $line;
}
```

```
$i = 1;
foreach $line (@lines) {
   print("$i:\t$line");
   $i++;
}
```

The program uses several new features, so let's go through the code slowly. The first command sets the value of $i to 0. (This is actually unnecessary, as Perl will automatically assign 0 to an uninitialized variable used in a numerical context.) The second command simply prints out the instructions for the user. The user will type a series of lines, each one terminated by a return. To signal an end to the input, the user enters a blank line. The program will read each of these lines into an array. It stops doing this when the current line has nothing in it.

Recall that reading from STDIN, results in a line terminated by a return. Thus an empty line actually has a single character in it: the terminating return. To check for the exit condition, the program must check that the line has more than one character. If it does, then the line is added to the buffer; if it doesn't, the program prints out whatever the contents of the array are at that point.

The next part of the program contains a while-structure for checking that the line has more than a return in it. The while-test here is rather complicated, as reflected in the nested parentheses. The string typed at the prompt is assigned to the variable $line. This assignment actually returns a value, the value assigned. That value is then passed to the function length(), which returns the length of its string argument. If the string is longer than one, if it is more than just a return, the while-condition is evaluated as true. The body of the while-structure assigns the value of $line to the current element of an array @lines. The current element is held in an integer variable $i, which is augmented immediately after it is used to assign the current element of the array.

When the user enters a blank line, the while-condition evaluates as false, and the structure is exited. The following foreach-structure is used to print out the contents of the array one by one. Each line of the array is prefixed by a counter and a tab (indicated in strings with the special character \t).

4.4   *Prompt Output*

We have actually already treated prompt output, presenting output at the prompt. This is done with the command print(). In point of fact, the print() command is an abbreviation for the command print(STDOUT), which prints its string output to the predefined "standard output" path. (This is generally defined as the screen.) The following program is thus identical to the preceding one:

promptex4.pl

```
print(STDOUT "Enter text below and a blank line to end.\n");
while ((length($line = <STDIN>)) > 1) {
    $lines[$i++] = $line;
}
$i = 1;
foreach $line (@lines) {
    print(STDOUT "$i:\t$line");
    $i++;
}
```

Notice how there is *not* a comma between STDOUT and the string argument to print(). When a function or command takes two arguments, they are generally separated by a comma, but not in this case.[7] This is a very common error, so try to avoid it.

Recall that there is another predefined output stream: STDERR, or "standard error". The print() command can also direct output to STDERR. The preceding program can thus be revised as follows with no apparent difference in behavior:

promptex5.pl

```
print(STDERR "Enter text below and a blank line to end.\n");
while ((length($line = <STDIN>)) > 1) {
    $lines[$i++] = $line;
}
$i = 1;
foreach $line (@lines) {
    print(STDERR "$i:\t$line");
    $i++;
}
```

However, the two last programs actually do have different behavior when we try to redirect the output of the programs to a file. Under Unix or in the DOS window, this is done by following the program name (and any command-line arguments) with > followed by the name of a file; for example, perl myprog.pl > myfile.txt. If output has been printed using STDOUT, then all the output from the program will end up in the file myfile.txt. If output has been printed using STDERR, then none of it will end up in the file.

In point of fact, what we want is for only the output of the foreach loop to end up in the file. The instructions to the user should not go to the file. To get this result, we use STDERR for the instructions to the user and STDOUT for the program's later output (since, as we already noted, STDOUT is the default case, we can leave any explicit handle out of the final print statement):

promptex6.pl

```perl
print(STDERR "Enter text below and a blank line to end.\n");
while ((length($line = <STDIN>)) > 1) {
    $lines[$i++] = $line;
}
$i = 1;
foreach $line (@lines) {
    print("$i:\t$line");
    $i++;
}
```

4.5   File IO

Let's now consider explicit file IO. The basic idea here is to read from and to files. This is a little more complex and a little more dangerous than the other IO cases we've considered. The danger is that you might accidentally over-write a file with something important in it. Therefore I *strongly* recommend that you do all your file IO practicing in a directory with nothing important in it.

Both file input and file output require pairing a file with a file handle, reading to or from that handle, and then closing it. You pair a file handle with a file with the open() command. This command takes two arguments: a file handle, and a string representing a file. For example, to read from a file myfile.txt, you would first pair it with a file handle FILE as follows: open(FILE, myfile.txt);.

It is very easy to make a mistake here. You might be in the wrong directory, the file you are trying to read might not be a readable file, and so on. If one of these things should happen, it is very difficult to diagnose. Your program will simply do nothing and you will bang your head against a wall until you remember that the file is actually named thefile.txt or some such.

To take care of this, you should add a test to the statement including the open() function. Typically, Perl programmers use an or structure with the die() command; for example, open(FILE, myfile.txt) or die("uhoh!\n");. If the open() command fails to open the file for any number of reasons, it will return false. This causes the statement after the or to be executed. The die() function prints out a string to the screen and then terminates the program immediately, without going through any other statements in the program. In this case, it prints out the uninformative message "uhoh!".[8]

Once a file is opened, once it is paired with a file handle, it can be read from. When Perl exits, it closes any open files, but it is a good habit to close these yourself. The reason you should is that when you write more complex programs, you may have any number of open file handles at the same time, and this can cause confusion on your part or problems for the Perl interpreter.

Closing a file is quite easy; you simply use the close() function. For example, to continue the example above, you would close the file as follows:

```
open(FILE, "myfile.txt") or die("uhoh!\n");
. . .
close(FILE);
```

This, of course, is not very useful in itself. We must now read from the file. We do this with angled brackets again. However, here, since a file can contain any number of lines, we must make provision for how to stop reading when the file has no more lines. The usual way to do this is with a while-loop. A very simple program exemplifying this follows. This program takes a filename as a command-line argument – for example, perl filex1.pl myfile.txt – and then prints the contents of that file to the screen line by line:

fileex1.pl

```
open(F, $ARGV[0]) or die("File couldn't be opened!\n");

while ($line = <F> ) {
    print($line);
}

close(F);
```

Here the filename is given by $ARGV[0] and taken from the command line. The open() command includes an or-die clause to take care of errors. The program is also terminated by a close() command to close the file.

The body of the program is a while-structure. The while-test itself reads a line of the file and assigns it to a variable $line. If this assignment succeeds – if the file still has lines in it to read – then the body of the loop is executed. If the while-test fails because there are no more lines in the file, then the body of the loop is exited. The body of the while-loop simply prints out the contents of $line. (Notice how the print() command does not include a \n since each line of the file is already terminated by return.)

Here's a second example. This program simply counts the number of lines and number of characters in a file using the length() command:

fileex2.pl

```
open(F, $ARGV[0]) or die("File couldn't be opened!\n");

while ($line = <F> ) {
    $chars += length($line);
    $lines++;
}

close(F);

print("lines: $lines, characters: $chars\n");
```

This program uses the same open(), close(), and while-structure. Inside the while-loop there are two statements. The first takes the length of the current line – calculated with length($line) – and adds it to a variable $chars. We use the operator +=, which takes the initial value of $chars, adds it to length $line, and then puts the total in $chars. This is thus shorthand for $chars = $chars + length($line);.[9] The second statement simply adds one to the variable $lines every time the loop is iterated; that is, once for each line of the file. Finally, the contents of the two counters are printed to the screen.

Let's now consider file output. File output is actually quite simple given what we know so far. First, a file must be paired with a file handle. Second, we use that file handle to direct output to the file. Finally, we close the file. The only new aspect is that we must specify that we are writing *to* a file. Moreover, we must indicate whether we are creating a new file (or overwriting an existing file) or whether we are appending to an existing file. This distinction is indicated in the string argument to open(). If we write to a new file (over-writing any already existing file with the same name), we would pass open() a string composed of a filename with a leading >; for example," > myfile.txt". On the other hand, if we wanted to append to an existing file, we would pass open() a filename with a leading >>; for example, ">> myfile.txt".

For example, the program we wrote on page 36 can be rewritten to print directly to a file. The following program exemplifies this:

fileex3.pl

```
print(STDERR "Enter text below and a blank line to end.\n");
while ((length($line = <STDIN>)) > 1) {
    $lines[$i++] = $line;
}
open(MYFILE, ">$ARGV[0]") or die("can't write to file!\n");
$i = 1;
foreach $line (@lines) {
```

```
    print(MYFILE "$i:\t$line");
    $i++;
}
close(MYFILE);
```

To write the output to a file myfile.txt if the program were called myprog.pl, you would type the following: perl myprog.pl myfile.txt. Notice how no > is required on the command line. Here myfile.txt is a command-line argument to myprog.pl. The program itself handles the redirection to the file.

The code is very similar to the earlier version of the program, except that we open a file handle MYFILE for output, using the command-line argument. The print() function uses this file handle in the while-loop to print to the file. Finally, the file is closed.

Notice that this program overwrites any existing file with the same name. You can see this by running the program with the same command-line file argument, but typing different contents each time. Examining the file after the second run of the program will show that only the material typed during the second run is in the file. This is true whether the redirection is handled on the command line, as on page 36, or in the Perl code as above.

If, instead, we want the program to *append* to an existing file, we can do that as well, either in Windows or DOS, or in the Perl code. To do this in Windows or DOS, the promptex5.pl program on page 35 can be invoked like this: perl myprog.pl >> myfile.txt.

To do this in the Perl code, the program above can be minimally revised as follows:

fileex4.pl

```
print(STDERR "Enter text below and a blank line to end.\n");
while ((length($line = <STDIN>)) > 1) {
    $lines[$i++] = $line;
}
open(MYFILE, ">> $ARGV[0]") or die("can't write to file!\n");
$i = 1;
foreach $line (@lines) {
    print(MYFILE "$i:\t$line");
    $i++;
}
close(MYFILE);
```

The only change here is that the > has been replaced with >>. Now if you run the program twice with the same command-line argument, it will *append* to the file, keeping a cumulative record of each run of the program.

This may all seem a little excessive, having several ways to redirect output to a file, but there are several reasons why we need to be able to do this from within Perl. First, since there is no command line on a Mac, we do not have the option of redirecting outside of Perl.[10] Second, we may not know the name of the file we want to redirect to when we start the program and therefore redirecting in Windows/Unix may not be an option even under those operating systems.

4.6   *Array Operations and Randomizing*

To show how we can make use of what we know so far to collect data about language, we will develop a program for collecting human subjects' intuitions about sentences. To do this effectively, though, we need some additional functions that allow us to randomize materials. This section introduces these.

4.6.1   Array operations

Recall from chapter 3 that arrays allow us to store a set of items in an indexed list of variables. Perl actually offers a set of functions that allow us to access and manipulate arrays easily: push(), pop(), shift(), unshift(), and splice(). As we've seen above, arrays are very convenient for storing the lines read from a file. These functions allow us to manipulate those lines easily.

The push() function adds an element – or list of elements – on the end of an array. The pop() function performs the complementary operation of removing an element from the end of the array (shortening the array correspondingly). The following simple program uses these to reverse the lines of a text file:

pushpopex.pl

```
if ($#ARGV != 0) { die("Enter a file on the command-line\n") }
open(F, $ARGV[0]) or die("File can't be opened\n");
while ($line = <F>) {
    push(@lines, $line);
}
close(F);
while ($#lines >= 0) {
    print(pop(@lines));
}
```

First, there is a check to make sure the user enters a command-line argument. Then, that argument – a filename – is opened for reading. Each line is pushed onto the end of an array @lines. Finally, a while-structure uses pop() to pop lines off the end of the array and print them.

We can actually do the same thing operating at the *beginning* of the array. The shift() function returns the first element from an array, while the unshift() function adds an element – or list of elements – to the front of the array. The following program has exactly the same effect as the preceding one:

shiftex.pl

```
if ($#ARGV != 0) { die("Enter a file on the command-line\n") }
open(F, $ARGV[0]) or die("File can't be opened\n");
while ($line = <F>) {
    unshift(@lines, $line);
}
close(F);
while ($#lines > = 0) {
    print(shift(@lines));
}
```

Finally, Perl offers one other array function for accessing *any* element of an array: splice(). This is an extremely useful function that can be called with any of one to four arguments:

splice(array, offset, length, list) Removes elements from array starting at offset for the number of elements specified by length, replacing them by the elements of the list.

splice(array, offset, length) Removes elements from array starting at offset for the number of elements specified by length.

splice(array, offset) Truncates the array from offset on.

splice(array) Removes everything in the array.

I exemplify the splice() function in the following section.

4.6.2   Randomizing

Perl provides the rand() function to generate random numbers. When invoked without an argument, it returns a random decimal between 0 and 1. When invoked with a (numerical) argument, it returns a decimal between 0 and the argument. Here is a simple program that returns however many random numbers the user requires in whatever range the user requires. The number of random numbers required is given as the first command-line argument, and the range of those numbers is given by the second:

ranex1.pl

```
$howmany = $ARGV[0];
$howbig = $ARGV[1];
for ($i = 0; $i < $howmany; $i++) {
    $r = rand($howbig);
    print("$i\t$r\n");
}
```

The $howmany variable stores the number of random numbers required; the $howbig variable stores the range of the random numbers. The for-loop keeps track of the number of random numbers generated.

In conjunction with the splice() function, we can use rand() to randomize an array of elements. The basic logic is as follows. Our program will start with an array of elements. Using rand(), we will randomly select one of those elements (using splice()) and push it onto the end of a second different array (using push() of course). We continue this until there are no more elements in the first array and all of them have been pushed onto the end of the second:

ranex2.pl

```
@digits = 0..9;
print("@digits\n");
while ($#digits > -1) {
    $r = rand($#digits+1);
    $digit = splice(@digits, $r, 1);
    push(@newdigits, $digit);
}
print("@newdigits\n");
```

This program exemplifies several new features, so let's go through it line by line. The first line creates an array @digits composed of the integers one through nine. Recall that the .. operator defines a list composed of the elements delimited by its two arguments.[11] The second statement prints out the elements of the array, confirming that the assignment did, in fact, work.

Next, there is a while-loop. This forces the statements within it to iterate until there are no more elements in the @digits array. Recall that the variable $#digits holds the last index of the array.

There are three statements in the while-loop. The first collects a random number between 0 and the last index of @digits, plus one. Thus, if there are eight elements in the array, the first statement will return a number between 0 and 9. The second splices off a random element from @digits and assigns it to $digit. This works because the splice() command coerces the number returned by rand() into an integer. Thus, if rand() were to generate 6.8, splice() would interpret it as 6.[12] Finally, $digit is pushed on the end of @newdigits.

4.7   Collecting Experimental Data

Let's now show how we can use what we've learned to write a little program to collect experimental data. The program is called expprog.pl, and it has a number of parts. It is the largest program we have constructed so far, but each bit is actually composed of familiar material.

The program will present stimuli one by one, collecting typed responses to each. The results are saved to a file at the end of the program. I'll go over the program in sections. First, there are a set of commands to initialize the program. The first command is a new one. The system() command executes the following command from the relevant operating system. In the example at hand, the cls command is an MS-DOS command to clear the screen.[13] The next two commands simply read the command-line arguments into two mnemonically named variables. The first holds the name of the file that the experimental materials are stored in, while the second holds the name of the file that the results will be appended to:

expprog.pl

```
system(cls);
$materials = $ARGV[0];
$results = $ARGV[1];
. . .
```

The next bit of code reads the experimental materials into an array @mats, using push(). It also creates an array @indices which holds just a sequence of integers mirroring the indices of the materials in the @mats array. This will be used to keep track of the original order of the items in the material file:

```
. . .
open(MATS, $materials) or die("Can't open materials file!\n");
$i = 0;
while ($line = <MATS>) {
    chomp($line);
    push(@mats, $line);
    push(@indices, $i);
    $i++;
}
close(MATS);
. . .
```

The next bit of code randomizes the materials into a new array @newmats. This bit is essentially identical to the ranex2.pl randomization program on page 42.

This snippet also keeps track of the original order of the materials in a separate array @newindices. We will use that array as a way of storing which item gets which response:

```
. . .
while ($#mats > -1) {
    $r = rand($#mats+1);
    $item = splice(@mats, $r, 1);
    $index = splice(@indices, $r, 1);
    push(@newmats, $item);
    push(@newindices, $index);
}
. . .
```

The next bit of code presents the materials, collects the responses, and saves the results to the results file. First, instructions are printed out. Then the results file is opened for appending results. There is then a for-loop to iterate through the randomized materials. Responses are collected and then printed to the results file:

```
. . .
print("For each of the following sentences, indicate
whether you find it acceptable or not.\n");
open(RES, ">> $results") or die("Can't save results!\n");
for ($i = 0; $i <= $#newmats; $i++) {
    print("$newmats[$i] (y/n): ");
    $response = <STDIN>;
    print(RES "$newindices[$i]\t$newmats[$i]\t$response");
}

close(RES);
```

Notice how each line printed to the results file includes the index from the @newindices array. In this way, we know which response goes with which item.

4.8   Summary

This chapter has covered the basic Perl IO system. We've discussed how to read from and write to the screen and files. In addition, we've discussed how to use command-line arguments. We've made extensive use of arrays as a way of storing information read from input, and this has necessitated some additional commands for manipulating arrays.

We have concluded with a program for collecting experimental language data that makes use of many of the ideas developed in the chapter.

4.9 Exercises

1. Write a program that does simple word translations from one language to another for some limited set of words. The user enters a word at an appropriate prompt and the program returns the appropriate translation at the prompt.
2. Write a program that prints out the even-numbered lines of a file in reverse order.
3. Write a program that uses *all* the IO options we've discussed.
4. Revise expprog.pl to collect reaction times.

Notes

[1] Though it is available as of MacOS 10.

[2] Traditionally, this is referred to as **console** output.

[3] Don't forget that the first index of an array is 0!

[4] The predefined handles are all capitalized, and this is an extremely useful habit to follow when you define your own handles.

[5] but this can be changed by resetting the appropriate special variable; see appendix C.

[6] In older versions of Perl, this command was unavailable. The older command, which you still see in very old code, is chop(). This removes *whatever* the final character of the string is.

[7] Technically, the handle is not an argument to the function, and that's why there is no comma.

[8] More specific information about the nature of the error can be obtained if the predefined variable $! is given as an argument to die(). This will return a number indicating the specific error.

[9] There are analogous shorthand operators for many other functions; for example, *=, -=, /=, .=, and so on.

[10] Macs do have a command line as of MacOS 10.

[11] This will, of course, only work if the arguments are part of a naturally ordered ascending sequence.

[12] Notice that the decimal isn't rounded off, but stripped off or ignored.

[13] If you are running this program under UNIX, you must replace cls with clear.

Chapter 5

Subroutines and Modules

We've now learned enough to make larger and really quite useful programs. However, we don't yet have enough to do that elegantly. In this chapter, I show how to break your programs up into useful and reusable components.

5.1 Japhs

One very interesting property of Perl is exemplified by the **japh** phenomenon. When the Perl language was just being introduced, there was a lot of activity on the relevant **usenet** groups. It got to be something of a joke for people posting to these groups on Perl to sign themselves as "just another Perl hacker". For some reason, people eventually started signing their emails with little Perl programs that would print out the "just another Perl hacker" phrase when run in Perl. Eventually, this escalated into people trying to outdo each other in writing the most convoluted Perl program to produce this phrase. Such programs are called japhs (for **Just Another Perl Hacker**).

Here's an example of a particularly obscure japh:

```
$_ = <<EOF; s#[-+]\d+#pack('C',$c+=$&)#eg; print;
+74+43-2+1-84+65+13+1+5-12-3+13-82+48+21+13-6-76+72-7+2+8-6+13-70
EOF
```

This particular example is due to Randal Schwartz, a now well-known author of numerous books on Perl.

The point of the example is that it is surprisingly easy to write completely unreadable code in Perl. Even a seasoned Perl professional would have difficulty in figuring out what the example above is supposed to do.

The fact that it is so easy to do this may have lots of causes. Most likely, it has to do with how easy the Perl language is to use. In any case, the upshot is that while it is always a good idea to write your programs in a readable fashion that makes it possible to reconstruct later what the program is supposed to do, this is even more crucial in Perl, where it is so easy to write mysterious-looking code.

5.2   Style and Comments

As you write larger and more complex programs, it becomes more and more essential that you write clear readable code. It is quite easy in Perl to write programs that simply look like raving gibberish – even to experienced Perl programmers! If you want your programs to be easy to maintain, easy to revise, easy to share with colleagues, then you should work at developing good programming style.

In this section, I make five specific recommendations for good programming style:[1]

- line breaks
- spaces and indentation
- comments
- mnemonic variable names
- avoiding command condensation

Let's go through these one by one.

The first thing is to make use of line breaks judiciously. Recall the ranex2.pl randomization program on page 42. The following program is formatted so that it breaks lines in completely different places, yet works just as well:

ranwrong1.pl

```
@digits =
0..9; print(
"@digits\n"); while
($#digits > -1) {$r = rand(
$#digits+1); $digit
= splice(@digits,
$r, 1); push(@newdigits, $digit);
} print("@newdigits\n");
```

Perl doesn't care where you break lines (except in strings); it can interpret this code just as easily as it interprets the earlier version.

For the human reader, though, this latter example is gibberish. It's extremely difficult to interpret. It's much easier to make errors when working with such illogically formatted code. Therefore, use line breaks to help make sense of your code.

Another thing to do is to make use of spaces and tabs appropriately. Again, Perl doesn't care how many spaces separate terms (except in strings). So these should be used judiciously. In addition, it is *extremely* helpful to use tabs to make program structure clear. For example, in the examples given so far, we have used tabs to show control structures. Again, here is a revision of the randomizing program that works just as well as the original, yet uses tabs in a completely unhelpful way:

ranwrong2.pl

```
@digits = 0..9;
print("@digits\n");
    while ($#digits > -1) {
$r = rand($#digits+1);
    $digit = splice(@digits, $r, 1);
push(@newdigits, $digit);
    }
print("@newdigits\n");
```

Here I've simply indented every other line, and the result is far less interpretable than the original.

Perl also allows for comments, lines of text that can be inserted in a program that are not interpreted by Perl, but that serve to remind the programmer of salient aspects of the code. Comments in Perl are indicated with # and go to the end of the line.[2] Here is yet another version of the randomizer program, this time with extensive comments:

ran-commented.pl

```
#randomization demo
@digits = 0..9;  #creates array of 10 numbers
print("@digits\n");
#loops over the @digits array
while ($#digits > -1) {
    #gets random number
    $r = rand($#digits+1);
    #pulls out random array element
    $digit = splice(@digits, $r, 1);
```

```
    #puts it in the new array
    push(@newdigits, $digit);
}
print("@newdigits\n");
```

The comments here are probably excessive, but serve to illustrate the syntax of Perl comments. Notice how comments can occur on their own line or on the right side of a line with code on it.

Another very important aspect of good style is using mnemonic variable names. For example, we can once again take our randomizer program and replace all the variables with very unintuitive variable names:

ranwrong3.pl

```
@a = 0..9;
print("@a\n");
while ($#a > -1) {
    $b = rand($#a+1);
    $c = splice(@a, $b, 1);
    push(@d, $c);
}
print("@d\n");
```

Here the names of the variables give *no* clue as to what they are used for. This makes it that much harder to figure out what the code is supposed to be doing, and that much easier to make mistakes. For example, should the last $c actually be $d?

Finally, it is extremely important to avoid what I'll term **command condensation**. This is when you collapse multiple commands into a single statement. Once again, this can be exemplified with a revision of the randomizer program:

ranwrong4.pl

```
@digits = 0..9;
print("@digits\n");
while ($#digits > -1) {
    push(@newdigits, splice(@digits, rand($#digits+1), 1));
}
print("@newdigits\n");
```

Here, we have collapsed the generation of the random number, splicing out the respective element from the first array, and pushing it onto the new array into a single statement. While this is clearly more economical in terms of space on the page, it results in far less clarity and should be avoided.

There are actually a number of other aspects to good programming style, but they involve aspects of Perl that we haven't treated yet. As we learn more about the language, I will point out places where programming style and clarity are most important.

5.3   The Anonymous Variables

One major threat to writing easy-to-read programs is **anonymous variables**. They are incredibly convenient, and virtually unavoidable when we discuss subroutines (in the next section). In addition, they are quite common in the code of experienced programmers, so if you ever hope to make use of other people's code, you need to understand them. In the interests of clarity, I will avoid them whenever possible.

Perl provides for a number of predefined **special variables**. Typically, they are composed of a $ followed by some punctuation mark. For example, the special variable $] holds the version number of the Perl interpreter. The following short program thus prints out the version of your Perl interpreter:

specex1.pl

```
print("version: $]\n");
```

This is only one of many. Many more – though not all! – are summarized in appendix C.

In this section, we discuss the special variable $_, the anonymous variable. Many (but not all!) functions in Perl that take an argument can be used without an argument. In that case, they automatically take $_ as their argument. Consider the following brief example:

anonex1.pl

```
open(F, $ARGV[0]) or die("Can't open file!\n");
while (<F>) {
   print();
}
close(F);
```

This program simply prints the contents of a file to the screen. It does so by making use of the anonymous variable $_. Notice that when the file handle F is read from with <F>, it is not explicitly assigned to any variable. In addition, the function print() does not have an argument. In both cases, Perl automatically inserts the anonymous variable $_. Thus, the above program is automatically converted into the following:

anonex2.pl

```
open(F, $ARGV[0]) or die("Can't open file!\n");
while ($_ = <F>) {
   print($_);
}
close(F);
```

In fact, you can enter and run the second program as is, but that would certainly detract from the utility of the anonymous variable. You would get the same functionality by replacing $_ with some named variable of your own; for example, $myLine. The value of $_ lies in the fact that it can be left out, that Perl automatically supplies it in certain contexts when an argument is required.

Most functions that take a single argument can default to the anonymous variable. In addition, as we've seen, reading from a file handle in a while-loop defaults to the anonymous variable as well. The pattern-matching operators treated in the next two chapters also default to the anonymous variable.

The last place it can be used is in foreach structures. Recall our first example of foreach on page 24, repeated below:

```
@verbs = ('run', 'jump', 'hit');
foreach $verb (@verbs) {
   print("$verb\n");
}
```

Very nearly the same functionality can be achieved with the anonymous variable, as follows:

anonex3.pl

```
@verbs = ('run', 'jump', 'hit');
foreach (@verbs) {
   print();
}
```

The only difference here is that the three verbs are printed on the same line with no spaces between them. The anonymous variable is interpolated after foreach, and after print(). The simplest way to print a return after each item, with minimal redundancy, and still making use of the anonymous variable, would be to actually include the anonymous variable overtly in the print() statement, as follows:

anonex4.pl

```
@verbs = ('run', 'jump', 'hit');
foreach (@verbs) {
   print("$_ \n");
}
```

Here, we are forced to use the anonymous variable overtly in the print() statement to get the return after each item. Notice though that we still don't need to use it overtly after the foreach.

The anonymous variable is an extremely convenient feature of Perl, but you should use it cautiously at the early stages. It is quite easy to generate very opaque code with it. Our goal at this stage is good workable code, not "maximally condensed" code.

5.4 *Subroutines*

Subroutines are an essential part of substantive programming. The basic idea is that reusable bits of code can be set off from the rest of the program and invoked with a simple command. Here's a rather simple example. Recall that to generate a new line at the end of a print() statement, we must terminate the print statement with \n, as in the program above. If we have a lot of print() statements, however, this can get tedious. The following program includes a separate subroutine to print a return at the end of each line:

subex1.pl

```
@verbs = ('run', 'jump', 'hit');
foreach (@verbs) {
   print();
   pn();
}

sub pn {
   print("\n");
}
```

Here's how this works. The command sub defines a subroutine with the name given, here pn(). The commands executed by this subroutine are given in the subsequent block, marked with curly braces. The subroutine is then invoked just like any other command.

Notice that the subroutine definition does *not* have to precede its use. That is, we can invoke the subroutine in the fourth line of the program even though it isn't defined until later in the program:

subex2.pl

```
sub pn {
    print("\n");
}

@verbs = ('run', 'jump', 'hit');
foreach (@verbs) {
    print();
    pn();
}
```

The examples given so far don't really show the full utility of subroutines. Where they really shine is when they provide some substantial *savings*, where some set of commands recurs more than once in a program and can therefore be replaced with a defined subroutine. We will see examples of this below.

Another extremely important property of subroutines is that – like primitive functions – they can return values. The following simple example illustrates:

subex3.pl

```
print("Enter a number: ");
$number = <STDIN>;
chomp($number);
print(times37());
pn();

sub times37 {
    return($number * 37);
}

sub pn {
    print("\n");
}
```

This program makes use of the pn() subroutine as well. In addition, it defines a new subroutine that calculates the value of $number multiplied by 37. It does this with the return command, followed by the value to be returned. The times37() function can be invoked just like any other, except that it returns a number, and can therefore be used anywhere a number might be used.

Subroutines can return any sort of value. For example, the following program exemplifies how a subroutine can return a value appropriate for testing in an if-structure:

subex4.pl

```perl
$num = $ARGV[0];
if (div37()) {
   print("Divisible by 37!\n");
} else {
   print("Not divisible by 37.\n");
}

sub div37 {
   if ($num % 37 == 0) {
      return(1);
   }
   return(0);
}
```

The subroutine tests if $num is divisible by 37. If it is, the subroutine returns 1. The return command immediately exits from the subroutine, so the final statement of the subroutine, return(0);, is only executed if the if-test is false. We could just as easily add an else clause, but although it is clearer, it isn't strictly necessary.

Notice too how the div37() subroutine can be invoked directly in the if-test. This is because Perl treats 1 as true, and 0 as false.

5.5   *Localizing Information*

Subroutines can get quite large. Eventually, you will find it necessary to use variables in your subroutines and it then becomes possible for the variables in each of your subroutines to conflict. Consider the following larger program:

subex5.pl

```perl
@letters = 'a'..$ARGV[0];
@numbers = 1..$ARGV[1];
printLetters();
```

```
sub printLetters {
   for ($i = 0; $i < = $#letters; $i++) {
      print("$letters[$i]");
      printNumbers();
      pn();
   }
}

sub printNumbers {
   for ($j = 0; $j <= $#numbers; $j++) {
      print("\t$numbers[$j]");
   }
}

sub pn {
   print("\n");
}
```

The program takes two command-line arguments, the first a letter, and the second a number. For each letter from "a" to the letter given, it prints out a row with that letter at the left. Each row is composed of a sequence of numbers from 1 to the number given as the second command-line argument. This display isn't very interesting in its own right, but provides a convenient representation of the looping behavior produced by the two subroutines that the program defines.

The first subroutine, printLetters(), prints out each letter in the letter sequence defined by @letters on its own line. This subroutine calls two others. One, pn(), simply prints out line breaks. The other, printNumbers() prints out the sequence of numbers defined by @numbers on the same line.

Both of the subroutines printNumbers() and printLetters() are constructed using for-structures. Notice that it is essential that the indices used in these structures be different. The following revision – where the indices are identical – will not work. It loops infinitely.

subwrong1.pl

```
@letters = 'a'..$ARGV[0];
@numbers = 1..$ARGV[1];
printLetters();

sub printLetters {
   for ($i = 0; $i <= $#letters; $i++) {
      print("$letters[$i]");
```

```
        printNumbers();
        pn();
    }
}


sub printNumbers {
    for ($i = 0; $i <= $#numbers; $i++) {
        print("\t$numbers[$i]");
    }
}


sub pn {
    print("\n");
}
```

The problem is that the inner loop in the printNumbers() subroutine resets $i to zero at each iteration of the outer loop (from the printLetters() subroutine). Hence, the outer loop will never terminate, because the value of $i will never reach $letters.

One solution is to make sure that none of the variables conflict (as in subex6.pl), but this doesn't solve the problem generally. It requires that you keep track of *all* the names of all your variables over your entire program, however large it might be.

Perl provides a simpler solution, however: **scoped variables**. Variables can be defined to exist in a specified domain. This is done with the my() command, which defines a variable only within the current block (curly braces) or file. The program above – the one that doesn't work – can be saved if the first mention of each $i is an argument of my(), as follows:

`subex6.pl`

```
@letters = 'a'..$ARGV[0];
@numbers = 1..$ARGV[1];
printLetters();


sub printLetters {
    for (my($i) = 0; $i <= $#letters; $i++) {
        print("$letters[$i]");
        printNumbers();
        pn();
    }
}
```

```
sub printNumbers {
   for (my($i) = 0; $i <= $#numbers; $i++) {
      print("\t$numbers[$i]");
   }
}

sub pn {
   print("\n");
}
```

What this does is define each variable only within the smallest enclosing block – here, the two subroutines. This means that the $i in printNumbers() is now distinct from the $i within printLetters(), and that setting the former to zero won't affect the latter.

Now you might be thinking that it would be a simpler matter to simply use different variables, and in the example at hand, that probably is the simplest solution. The problem is that as your programs get larger and larger, it becomes harder and harder to keep track of what variable names you've already used in earlier parts of the program. The my() command avoids this problem.

5.6 *Arguments*

So far, our subroutines have operated on the variables that are globally available, but we can invoke our subroutines on specific arguments. This allows us to control the flow of data in a program more carefully, and makes possible **recursive** subroutines.

Arguments can be given to a subroutine the same way they are given to any other predefined function, either in parentheses or directly following the subroutine name, separated by commas. These arguments are automatically put into the predefined array @_. Using these arguments is as simple as examining this array. The only tricky part is that – like $_ – the @_ array can be used anonymously. I will demonstrate this below.

Let's first consider a very simple example. This program is a revision of the subex3.pl program on page 53 (to focus in on relevant details, the pn() subroutine has been eliminated):

subex7.pl

```
print("Enter a number: ");
$number = <STDIN>;
chomp($number);
print(times37($number), "\n");
```

```
sub times37 {
   my($num) = $_[0];
   return($num * 37);
}
```

Here, the times37() subroutine is constructed to take an argument. When the subroutine is invoked, the argument is placed in parentheses after the subroutine name. In the subroutine itself, the argument is available as the first element of the array @_. This is assigned to a local variable which is declared with the my() command.

Notice too that $num is introduced with my() since $num is only used within the times37() subroutine.

Note also that @_ is an anonymous variable, like $_. Thus, the following revision of the above program will also work:

subex8.pl

```
print("Enter a number: ");
$number = <STDIN>;
chomp($number);

sub times37 {
   my($num) = shift();
   return($num * 37);
}

print(times37($number), "\n");
```

Here the local variable $num is assigned the value of the first argument to times37() with the shift() command. Since shift() is given no argument, it takes the anonymous array @_ as an argument, shifting the first (and only) element of the array off, and assigning it to $num.

Subroutines can take multiple arguments as well. The following rather silly example takes two string arguments and prints out a message tailored to its arguments:

subex9.pl

```
sub thank {
   my($name) = shift();
   my($food) = shift();
   print("Dear $name:\nThank you for the $food!\n\n");
}
```

```
thank("Joe", "donuts");
thank("Diane", "cookies");
```

Here, the subroutine thank() is invoked twice with different arguments. It collects those arguments from the anonymous array @_ by invoking shift() twice.

It is, of course, also possible to dump the contents of the array as a list. The following revision of the preceding program exemplifies:

subex10.pl

```
sub thank {
    my ($name, $food) = @_;
    print("Dear $name:\nThank you for the $food!\n\n");
}

thank("Joe", "donuts");
thank("Diane", "cookies");
```

Here the local variables $name and $food are placed in **list context,** by placing them in parentheses. The elements of the @_ array are then assigned one by one to the elements in parentheses.

In fact, it is possible for a subroutine to have an indeterminate number of arguments, as exemplified in the following program. This program is like the preceding one, except that it has a slightly different result depending on the number of arguments it is given:

subex11.pl

```
sub thank {
    my ($name, $food);
    if ($#_ == -1) {
        $name = "Joe";
        $food = "donuts";
    } elsif ($#_ == 0) {
        $name = shift();
        $food = "donuts";
    } else {
        $name = shift();
        $food = shift();
        foreach (@_) {
            $food = $food . " and " . $_;
        }
    }
```

```
    }
    print("Dear $name:\nThank you for the $food!\n\n");
}

thank("Joe", "donuts");
thank("Diane", "cookies");
thank("Puck", "pizza", "apricots", "asparagus");
```

If the subroutine is invoked with no arguments, it sets $name to "Joe" and $food to "donuts", and prints out the same message as before. If it's given a single argument, then it takes that argument as $name and sets $food to "donuts" again. If it's given two arguments, it sets the variable accordingly. If it's given more than two arguments, then it assigns the first to $name and all the rest to $food as a conjoined list.

It does this with an if-structure, which produces different results depending on the size of the anonymous array, which is stored, as we expect, in a variable $#_. Depending on the value of $#_, differing numbers of arguments are peeled off with shift(). The last case is the most interesting because the foreach-structure makes use of both the anonymous array @_ and the anonymous variable $_. Recall that the values that foreach iterates on are automatically assigned to $_ unless a specific variable name is given.

As a final example of a subroutine, let's consider an example of **recursion,** an example where the subroutine is defined in terms of itself. The particular example below calculates the factorial of a number (written *n!*). Recall from page 22 that the factorial of a number is calculated by multiplying all the numbers between it and zero together. For example, the factorial of 5 is $5 \times 4 \times 3 \times 2 \times 1 = 120$. The factorial of 0 is defined as 1 ($0! = 1$), and the factorial of a negative number is undefined:

recur1.pl

```
my($data) = fac($ARGV[0]);
print("The factorial of $ARGV[0] is $data\n");

sub fac {
    my($out);
    my($in) = shift();
    if ($in < 0) {
        $out = "undefined";
    } elsif ($in == 0) {
        $out = 1;
    } else {
```

```
        $out = $in * fac($in-1);
    }
    return($out);
}
```

The body of the program is an if/else structure based on the size of the argument. If the argument is less than zero, the subroutine returns "undefined". If the number is zero, the subroutine returns 1. The recursive case occurs when the number is greater than 0. In that case, the subroutine returns the number multiplied times the result of applying the subroutine to the number minus one.

For example, if the subroutine is invoked with the number 3, the if-structure takes us to the recursive case, telling us that fac(3) should return 3 times fac(2). That in turn tells us that fac(2) should return 2 times fac(1). Again, we are taken to the recursive block of the subroutine, which tells us that fac(1) should return 1 times fac(0). Finally, the last call to fac() takes us to a nonrecursive block of the if-structure. The upshot of all this is that 3! is defined like this: $3! = 3 \times 2! = 3 \times 2 \times 1! = 3 \times 2 \times 1 \times 0! = 3 \times 2 \times 1 \times 1$.

5.7   Collecting More Experimental Data

In section 4.7, we developed a program to collect experimental data. In this section, we revise that program making use of subroutines, using my() to localize variables where possible.

The following program exemplifies this. Compare it with the original program, beginning on page 43. The original program was broken up into conceptual units that were marked simply by spacing in the program. In the following program, these conceptual units have each been put in separate subroutines.

In addition, some of the variables declared are only really needed within one or another of the subroutines; they are not needed outside of the subroutine they are declared in. In these cases, the relevant variables are now marked with my().

`expprog2.pl`

```
initialize();
readmaterials();
randomizemats();
presentmats();
```

```
#does initialization; replace "cls" with "clear" for unix
sub initialize {
    system(cls);
    $materials = $ARGV[0];
    $results = $ARGV[1];
}


#reads materials from file into array
sub readmaterials {
    my($line);
    open(MATS, $materials) or die("Can't open materials file!\n");
    my($i) = 0;
    while ($line = <MATS>) {
        chomp($line);
        push(@mats, $line);
        push(@indices, $i);
        $i++;
    }
    close(MATS);
}


#randomizes materials, saving initial indices
sub randomizemats {
    my ($r, $item, $index);
    while ($#mats > -1) {
        $r = rand($#mats+1);
        $item = splice(@mats, $r, 1);
        $index = splice(@indices, $r, 1);
        push(@newmats, $item);
        push(@newindices, $index);
    }
}


#present materials, saving results
sub presentmats {
    my($response);
    print("For each of the following sentences, indicate
whether you find it acceptable or not.\n");
    open(RES, ">>$results")or die("Can't save results!\n");
    for (my($i) = 0; $i <= $#newmats; $i++) {
        print("$newmats[$i] (y/n): ");
        $response = <STDIN>;
```

```
        print(RES "$newindices[$i]\t$newmats[$i]\t$response");
    }
    close(RES);
}
```

The following table shows which variables need to be shared across which subroutines and which are local to only one subroutine. The checklists on the right show which subroutines use which variables:

Variable	Local	init.	read.	rand.	pres.
$materials	No	Yes	Yes		
$results	No	Yes			Yes
$line	Yes		Yes		
$i	Yes		Yes		
@mats	No		Yes	Yes	
@indices	No		Yes	Yes	
$r	Yes			Yes	
$item	Yes			Yes	
$index	Yes			Yes	
@newmats	No			Yes	Yes
@newindices	No			Yes	Yes
$response	Yes				Yes
$i	Yes				Yes

Variables are declared local with my() when they appear in only one sub-routine. The only exception is $i, which is referred to in readmaterials() and presentmats(). Note, however, that the *value* of $i is not carried over between the subroutines. Instead, presentmats() reinitializes $i to zero at its first invocation. Since the value of $i doesn't carry over, these can be treated as *distinct* local variables. The my() command allows this.

5.8 Modules

The whole point of subroutines is to separate out reusable bits of code. This can be much more efficient, for example, when the same command sequence would otherwise be called again and again. It can also be conceptually super-ior, when separating your code into separate subroutines makes clearer the division of labor in your program.

This latter point may sound fairly abstract, but it translates into real-world benefits. Separating your code into separate subroutines helps make the

different tasks your program is taking care of clearer, and that helps *you* –
the programmer – to see how best to program those different tasks.

There is, in fact, another level of conceptual separation available in Perl.
So far, we have used subroutines as a way of separating out some sequence
of commands that might otherwise be repeated in some program. What about
the case of some sequence of commands that might otherwise be repeated in
several *different* programs? Imagine, for example, that you have several different programs that each need access to factorials? One possibility is to copy
the fac() subroutine into each of them. This is problematic for two reasons.

First, this is inefficient, as you have to repeat the same bit of code again
and again.

Second, imagine you discover a more efficient way to calculate factorials. If
you did, you would then have to go to each of the programs that uses the
fac() subroutine and change them all separately. This is inefficient and there
is a reasonable chance of error.

Perl **modules** provide a solution to this problem. The basic idea is that bits
of code can be put in separate *files*, which are available to any program that
you tell where that file is. Such files are termed modules, and are marked with
the file extension .pm.

Here's how it works. You put the code that you want access to in a file with
the extension .pm. Second, you put a package declaration at the beginning of
the module file. The package statement takes a single argument which should
match the name of the module file. Third, you make sure that the last line of
the file is a line that returns as true; this is usually done by making the last
line of the module file 1;. Finally, you invoke the module in your program
with the use statement. Let's revise the subex11.pl program on page 59 as an
example. First, we extract the subroutine thank() and put it in a separate file,
which we call Modex1.pm:

Modex1.pm

```perl
package Modex1;

sub thank {
  my ($name, $food);
  if ($#_ == -1) {
    $name = "Joe";
    $food = "donuts";
  } elsif ($#_ == 0) {
    $name = shift();
    $food = "donuts";
  } else {
    $name = shift();
    $food = shift();
```

```
      foreach (@_) {
         $food = $food . " and " . $_;
      }
   }
   print("Dear $name:\nThank you for the $food!\n\n");
}


1;
```

This file also includes a final line which is guaranteed to return true.

The second file in this program is the one that calls the module file. It includes all the rest of the original program, aside from the subroutine definition. In addition, it includes the use statement, which takes the name of the module file as an argument (*without* the .pm extension). Finally, anything called from the Modex1 module must be *qualified* with the module name, separated by two colons; for example, Modex1::thank():

modcallex1.pl

```
use Modex1;

Modex1::thank("Joe", "donuts");
Modex1::thank("Diane", "cookies");
Modex1::thank("Puck", "pizza", "apricots", "asparagus");
```

This allows us to reuse the thank() subroutine in any program we like. In fact, as we will see in subsequent sections, we can put whatever we like into a module; we are not limited to a single subroutine.

5.9 *Multidimensional Arrays*

The next logical step is to separate our subroutines into separate modules. This will allow us to write new code to run new types of experiments that make use of the modules we have written.

To do this, however, we need to make some changes to the subroutines we have written. In particular, readmaterials(), randomizemats(), and presentmats() need to be revised so that the array variables they manipulate are passed as arguments, rather than being available globally. There are several ways to do this, but the simplest is to collapse the two arrays into a single **multidimensional array**.[3]

In section 3.4, we introduced one-dimensional arrays. An array is a group of variables that have a single name. Each individual variable in the array is identified with an integer index. Thus we might have a one-dimensional array @hat with three component variables: $hat[0], $hat[1], and $hat[2].

A multidimensional array is simply an array of arrays. Each member of the main array is itself an array. If the array is two-dimensional, then each variable in the multidimensional array would be identified with *two* indices. The first index would indicate which subarray the variable is in. The second index would indicate which variable of the subarray is being referred to. For example, we could define a two-dimensional array @chair with three subarrays, each containing two variables. The individual elements would then be referred to as follows: $chair[0][0], $chair[0][1], $chair[1][0], $chair[1][1], $chair[2][0], and $chair[2][1]. The logic of a two-dimensional array is perhaps best seen in a table:

	First subarray element	Second subarray element
First subarray	$chair[0][0]	$chair[0][1]
Second subarray	$chair[1][0]	$chair[1][1]
Third subarray	$chair[2][0]	$chair[2][1]

Another way to think of a two-dimensional array is to think of it as defining a plane on which the individual variables are located. Each variable is accessed in terms of its *x,y*-coordinates on that plane.[4]

Multidimensional arrays are extremely handy data structures. They allow you to assign subgroups to a larger set of data. For example, imagine you wanted to keep a database of language names, organized in terms of language families. This can be readily accomplished with a multidimensional array. The basic idea is to use the first index of the multidimensional array to store language families. The second index is used to store individual language names. Here's a very simple program that collects the names of language families, and individual languages. The user is prompted to enter the names of language families, and then specific language names. Hitting return at either prompt either moves on to a new language family, or ends the user input phase of the program. The program then simply iterates through the multidimensional array printing out each language family, along with the languages that belong to it.

The logic of the program is straightforward. There are two nested while-structures for reading in the names of language families and languages respectively. The while-tests test for whether the user has entered a string or only hit return. Notice how the name of each language family occurs in the zeroth position of the second index:

languagefamily.pl

```perl
print("Language family program\n");

$theprompt = "Enter a language family> ";
$otherprompt = "Enter a specific language> ";
$i = 0;

print($theprompt);

while (($family = <STDIN>) ne "\n") {
    chomp($family);
    $j = 0;
    $family[$i][$j++] = $family;
    print($otherprompt);
    while (($language = <STDIN>) ne "\n") {
        chomp($language);
        $family[$i][$j++] = $language;
        print($otherprompt);
    }
    print($theprompt);
    $i++;
}

for ($i = 0; $i <= $#family; $i++) {
    print("Family:\t$family[$i][0]\n");
    for ($j = 1; $j <= $#{$family[$i]}; $j++) {
        print("Language:\t$family[$i][$j]\n");
    }
}
```

There are two things to notice about this code. First, notice how the index maxima for the two indices of @family are represented. For the first index, the usual syntax applies: $#family. For the second index, we must specify what the *first* index is to determine which **slice** of the array we want to determine the index maximum of. For example, to determine the maximum for the second subarray of @family, we use $#{$family[1]}. This may seem a little convoluted until one notes that each **slice** of the array can have different numbers of elements. In other words, the program allows for each language family to have different numbers of component languages. Hence, we need to be able to determine an index maximum for any one of them.

Here is the kind of input–output pattern that the program produces (user input is indicated in bold here):

```
> perl languagefamily.pl
Language family program
Enter a language family> Italic
Enter a specific language> French
Enter a specific language> Italian
Enter a specific language>
Enter a language family> Germanic
Enter a specific language> English
Enter a specific language> Dutch
Enter a specific language> German
Enter a specific language>
Enter a language family> Athabaskan
Enter a specific language> Navajo
Enter a specific language> Apache
Enter a specific language>
Enter a language family>
Family: Italic
Language: French
Language: Italian
Family: Germanic
Language: English
Language: Dutch
Language: German
Family: Athabaskan
Language: Navajo
Language: Apache
>
```

5.10   *Localizing Variables*

We can use multidimensional arrays to localize the variables that the experimental program manipulates. We've seen that a subroutine can take multiple arguments; the problem is that they can return only a single value.[5] Several of the subroutines in expprog2.pl manipulate *several* variables. Hence, to turn these into local variables, to turn them into variables that are returned by each subroutine, we need a mechanism to have several of them returned at once.

In each case, the relevant variables are parallel arrays, arrays that can be readily compressed into multidimensional arrays. These, in turn, can be passed from subroutine to subroutine via arguments and return statements. The following program shows how this is done. I go through it in stages.

The first lines of the program simply call the subsequent subroutines using @ARGV as arguments. The second call uses the output of each of the various subroutines as input to the others. The readmaterials() subroutine takes a filename as an argument and returns an array of items. These items are then passed as an argument to randomizemats(), which returns a multidimensional array. That in turn is taken as an argument to presentmats(), which presents the materials, saving the results in a filename given by its first argument:

expprog3.pl

```
initialize(@ARGV);
presentmats($ARGV[1],randomizemats(readmaterials($ARGV[0])));
. . .
```

The first subroutine is initialize(). This clears the screen and checks the number of arguments given on the command line:

```
. . .
#does initialization; replace "cls" with "clear" for unix
sub initialize {
    my(@args) = @_;
    system(cls);
    if ($#args != 1) {
        die("usage:\tperl expprog3.pl materialsfile resultsfile\n");
    }
}
. . .
```

The next subroutine is readmaterials(). It reads through the materials file line by line, storing each item in the first slice of a multidimensional array. The second slice of the array is used for storing the item number. This may appear to be redundant, as the item numbers stored are minimally different from the indices used to store them. However, when the materials are randomized in the next step, these item numbers will be critical in recovering the original order of the items:

```
. . .
#reads materials from file into array
sub readmaterials {
    my(@mats);
    my($line);
    my($matsfile) = shift();
    open(MATS, $matsfile) or die("Can't open materials file!\n");
    my($i) = 0;
    while ($line = <MATS>) {
        chomp($line);
        push(@{$mats[0]}, $line);
```

```
      push(@{$mats[1]}, $i);
      $i++;
   }
   close(MATS);
   return(@mats);
}
. . .
```

The randomizemats() subroutine randomizes both slices of the multi-dimensional array @mats. Since both slices of the array are randomized as a pair, the original position of the element is recoverable from the second member of each pair. The randomizemats() subroutine returns the multi-dimensional array with its final return() statement:

```
. . .
#randomizes materials, saving initial indices
sub randomizemats {
   my ($r, $item, $index);
   my(@mats) = @_;
   my(@newmats);
   while ($#{$mats[0]}> -1) {
      $r = rand($#{$mats[0]}+1);
      $item = splice(@{$mats[0]}, $r, 1);
      $index = splice(@{$mats[1]}, $r, 1);
      push(@{$newmats[0]}, $item);
      push(@{$newmats[1]}, $index);
   }
   return(@newmats);
}
. . .
```

Finally, the presentmats() subroutine presents the items one by one, saving responses, items, and the original item numbers to a file given as its first argument:

```
. . .
#present materials, saving results
sub presentmats {
   my($response);
   my($resfile) = shift();
   my(@mats) = @_;
   print("For each of the following sentences, indicate
whether you find it acceptable or not.\n");
   open(RES, ">>$resfile") or die("Can't save results!\n");
```

```
   for (my($i) = 0; $i <= $#{$mats[0]}; $i++) {
      print("$mats[0][$i] (y/n): ");
      $response = <STDIN>;
      print(RES "$mats[1][$i]\t$mats[0][$i]\t$response");
   }
   close(RES);
}
```

5.11   Subroutines to Modules

Putting these separate subroutines into separate modules is now quite simple. Each subroutine goes in a separate file. The files end with the extension .pm and the text of the file begins with a package declaration that matches the filename. For example, we put the initialize() subroutine in a file called Exp_init.pm that begins with a statement package Exp_init;.

In addition, as already discussed above, each module file must end with a statement that evaluates to true. This is done by making 1; the last line of each module file.

Here are the four module files created from the four subroutines in the previous section:

Exp_init.pm

```
package Exp_init;

#does initialization; replace "cls" with "clear" for unix
sub initialize {
   my(@args) = @_;
   system(cls);
   if ($#args != 1) {
      die("usage:\tperl expprog4.pl materialsfile resultsfile\n");
   }
}

1;
```

Exp_read.pm

```
package Exp_read;

#reads materials from file into array
sub readmaterials {
   my(@mats);
   my($line);
```

```perl
   my($matsfile) = shift();
   open(MATS, $matsfile) or die("Can't open materials file!\n");
   my($i) = 0;
   while ($line = <MATS>) {
      chomp($line);
      push(@{$mats[0]}, $line);
      push(@{$mats[1]}, $i);
      $i++;
   }
   close(MATS);
   return(@mats);
}

1;
```

Exp_rand.pm

```perl
package Exp_rand;

#randomizes materials, saving initial indices
sub randomizemats {
   my ($r, $item, $index);
   my(@mats) = @_;
   my(@newmats);
   while ($#{$mats[0]}> -1) {
      $r = rand($#{$mats[0]}+1);
      $item = splice(@{$mats[0]}, $r, 1);
      $index = splice(@{$mats[1]}, $r, 1);
      push(@{$newmats[0]}, $item);
      push(@{$newmats[1]}, $index);
   }
   return(@newmats);
}

1;
```

Exp_pres.pm

```perl
package Exp_pres;

#present materials, saving results
sub presentmats {
   my($response);
   my($resfile) = shift();
```

```
    my(@mats) = @_;
    print("For each of the following sentences, indicate
whether you find it acceptable or not.\n");
    open(RES, ">>$resfile") or die("Can't save results!\n");
    for (my($i) = 0; $i <= $#{$mats[0]}; $i++) {
        print("$mats[0][$i] (y/n): ");
        $response = <STDIN>;
        print(RES "$mats[1][$i]\t$mats[0][$i]\t$response");
    }
    close(RES);
}

1;
```

Making use of these modules is also straightforward. We simply include a use statement at the beginning of the calling program, and then invoke the methods by naming the package overtly. The following revision of the expprog.pl program shows how this works:

expprog4.pl

```
use Exp_init;
use Exp_read;
use Exp_pres;
use Exp_rand;

Exp_init::initialize(@ARGV);

Exp_pres::presentmats($ARGV[1],
    Exp_rand::randomizemats(Exp_read::readmaterials($ARGV[0])));
```

5.12 Using Exporter

If we write a package that we expect to use a great deal, it is rather an inconvenience to have to name the package each time we call a subroutine from it. We can avoid this by making use of the standard Exporter module. Adding a few lines of code to each module file will enable us to use its subroutines without naming the package overtly every time one of the subroutines is invoked.

The Exporter module is part of every Perl distribution. Precisely how it does what it does and what the statements we must include mean is something that we won't be covering until appendix A. We can still make use of it to simplify how module subroutines are called. The basic idea is that each module we write should itself use the Exporter module. In addition, each module should include two additional statements. The first specifies that the relevant module is an "instance" of the Exporter **class**. The second statement stipulates which of your module's subroutines are available when the module is invoked:

```
package Mypackage;
use Exporter;
@ISA = "Exporter";
@EXPORT = ("mysubroutine", "myothersubroutine");
. . .
```

Here you would replace Mypackage with the name of your package and mysubroutine, and so on with the names of the subroutines you are exporting.

Here are the four modules now rewritten to invoke the Exporter module:

Exp_init2.pm

```
package Exp_init2;

use Exporter;
@ISA = ("Exporter");
@EXPORT = ("initialize");

#does initialization; replace "cls" with "clear" for unix
sub initialize {
    my(@args) = @_;
    system(cls);
    if ($#args != 1) {
        die("usage:\tperl expprog5.pl materialsfile resultsfile\n");
    }
}

1;
```

Exp_read2.pm

```
package Exp_read2;

use Exporter;
@ISA = ("Exporter");
@EXPORT = ("readmaterials");
```

```
#reads materials from file into array
sub readmaterials {
    my(@mats);
    my($line);
    my($matsfile) = shift();
    open(MATS, $matsfile) or die("Can't open materials file!\n");
    my($i) = 0;
    while ($line = <MATS>) {
        chomp($line);
        push(@{$mats[0]}, $line);
        push(@{$mats[1]}, $i);
        $i++;
    }
    close(MATS);
    return(@mats);
}

1;
```

Exp_rand2.pm

```
package Exp_rand2;

use Exporter;
@ISA = ("Exporter");
@EXPORT = ("randomizemats");

#randomizes materials, saving initial indices
sub randomizemats {
    my ($r, $item, $index);
    my(@mats) = @_;
    my(@newmats);
    while ($#{$mats[0]}> -1) {
        $r = rand($#{$mats[0]}+1);
        $item = splice(@{$mats[0]}, $r, 1);
        $index = splice(@{$mats[1]}, $r, 1);
        push(@{$newmats[0]}, $item);
        push(@{$newmats[1]}, $index);
    }
    return(@newmats);
}

1;
```

Exp_pres2.pm

```
package Exp_pres2;

use Exporter;
@ISA = ("Exporter");
@EXPORT = ("presentmats");


#present materials, saving results
sub presentmats {
  my($response);
  my($resfile) = shift();
  my(@mats) = @_;
  print("For each of the following sentences, indicate
whether you find it acceptable or not.\n");
  open(RES, ">>$resfile") or die("Can't save results!\n");
  for (my($i) = 0; $i <= $#{$mats[0]}; $i++) {
    print("$mats[0][$i] (y/n): ");
    $response = <STDIN>;
    print(RES "$mats[1][$i]\t$mats[0][$i]\t$response");
  }
  close(RES);
}


1;
```

Calling these modules is then quite simple. The following program is a revision of the expprog.pl program that takes advantage of the fact that the modules now use the Exporter module:

expprog5.pl

```
use Exp_init2;
use Exp_read2;
use Exp_pres2;
use Exp_rand2;

initialize(@ARGV);

presentmats($ARGV[1], randomizemats(readmaterials($ARGV[0])));
```

5.13 *Taking Advantage of Separate Modules*

The advantage of separate modules is that they can be easily reused for different programs. In this section, we develop another experiment type, taking advantage of the modules we have already written for the experiment above.

Imagine you want to collect people's intuitions about the number of syllables in words. The number of syllables for some word types is quite straightforward. For example, *table* has two syllables, *potato* three, and *intercalation* five. However, some words are a little more difficult to characterize. For example, does *flour* have one or two syllables? Quite reasonably, you might believe that the spelling will affect how people syllabify words like *flour* versus *flower*, and you want to test this experimentally.

The task will be quite similar to the preceding one. Subjects will be presented with a randomized set of words and asked to indicate how many syllables each word has.

Let's make this more challenging though. Let's add in some code to *insure* that subjects actually respond with a number. If subjects respond with something other than a number, then they will be prompted again to enter a number.

We can accomplish this straightforwardly with minimal revisions to the experimental code we've already written. We will leave most of the modules intact: Exp_init2.pm, Exp_read2.pm, and Exp_rand2.pm. Substantive revisions will only go in the Exp_pres2.pm module, renamed Exp_pres3.pm. The expprog5.pl program must be revised as well to call this new module:

expprog6.pl

```
use Exp_init2;
use Exp_read2;
use Exp_pres3;
use Exp_rand2;

initialize(@ARGV);

presentmats($ARGV[1], randomizemats(readmaterials($ARGV[0])));
```

Most of the changes for the new experiment type are straightforward. The instructions must be different and subjects must be prompted to enter a number, rather than "yes" or "no" to each item.

To check that subjects actually enter a number, we use a while-loop. The subject's response is saved in a variable $response. If it is not a number, the subject is prompted again. To check that the response is actually a number, we use a trick. By adding something to $response, we force Perl to treat it as a number. If it is, in fact, a nonnumeric string, then Perl treats it as 0. We then simply check whether the result of adding 0 to $response is greater than 0.[6] Here is the code for the new module:

Exp_pres3.pm

```perl
package Exp_pres3;

use Exporter;
@ISA = ("Exporter");
@EXPORT = ("presentmats");

#present materials, saving results
sub presentmats {
    my($response);
    my($resfile) = shift();
    my(@mats) = @_;
    print("For each of the following words, indicate
the number of syllables.\n");
    open(RES, ">>$resfile") or die("Can't save results!\n");
    for (my($i) = 0; $i <=$#{$mats[0]}; $i++) {
        print($mats[0][$i]);
        $response = getResp();
        print(RES "$mats[1][$i]\t$mats[0][$i]\t$response");
    }
    close(RES);
}

sub getResp {
    my($response) = 0;
    while ($response < 1) {
        print(" (enter a number): ");
        $response = <STDIN>;
        $response += 0;
    }
    return($response);
}

1;
```

All the interesting new action is in the getResp() subroutine. The only other thing to note is that this new subroutine is *not* exported in the @EXPORT array at the beginning of the module. This is because the new subroutine is invoked only inside its own module; there is no need to make it available outside the module.

5.14 Summary

We've covered a lot of important topics in this chapter. We began by discussing Perl style and comments. We have already reached the point at which it's possible to write fairly complex programs. Anything you can do to help keep your programs comprehensible will benefit you in the long run.

We next went on to treat the anonymous variable, probably one of the most convenient features of Perl, but also one of the most dangerous to easy-to-read code. The anonymous variable is essential to understanding arguments to subroutines.

We next treated subroutines, showing how they provide a means of simplifying and organizing larger programs. We showed how subroutines can take arguments and how they can return values. In addition, we showed how subroutines allow for recursive algorithms.

Finally, we treated Perl modules, a more extreme way of organizing your programs. Modules allow you to reuse subroutines in different programs.

5.15 Exercises

1. Add appropriate comments to the expprog6.pl program – and all the relevant modules.
2. Find a language-related problem that can be solved using a recursive algorithm in Perl.
3. Propose and implement another experiment type that extends the expprog network of modules.

Notes

[1] There are some Perl style standards, only some of which I use here. These can be seen in the standard Perl documentation with the command perldoc perlstyle.
[2] Perl thus does use line breaks in interpreting comments.
[3] Another method is to make use of references, but this is a very complicated topic that I defer to appendix A.
[4] It is, in fact, possible to define any number of dimensions in an array, but we will not need more than two in this book.
[5] This is actually not quite true. There is no problem specifying that a subroutine return a *list* of elements. The problem is when those elements include arrays. A list of arrays is automatically treated as a flattened list of elements. There are two solutions to this: multidimensional arrays, as in the text, or references, as in appendix A.
[6] We will see in the next chapter that there are other more efficient ways to determine if something is a number.

Chapter 6

Regular Expressions

Probably the most useful aspect of Perl for language-related programming is its regular expression syntax. This chapter (and the next) show how regular expressions can be constructed to handle the most intricate kinds of pattern-matching, and how this is useful for language researchers. Several programs demonstrating the utility of regular expressions are given at the end of the chapter.

6.1 Basic Syntax

Regular expressions are a way of characterizing some set of strings. Specifically, a regular expression is built on three primitive operations: **concatenation**, **union**, and **Kleene star**. Patterns are matched in Perl by first characterizing the pattern to be matched in terms of a regular expression, and then using the pattern-matching syntax to test whether some string matches the pattern.

For example, to test whether a string contains the substring abc, we use this syntax: $string =~ m/abc/;. This expression returns true or false, depending on whether $string contains abc. The regular expression itself is enclosed in slashes, preceded by an (optional) m. The pattern is bound to the string with =~. The following very simple program shows how every line in a file that matches some pattern – given as a command-line argument – can be printed out:

pat1.pl

```
open(F, $ARGV[1]) or die("Can't open file!\n");

while ($line = <F>) {
    if ($line =~ m/$ARGV[0]/) {
```

```
        print($line);
    }
}

close(F);
```

The m is optional, so the following code is exactly equivalent:

pat2.pl

```
open(F, $ARGV[1]) or die("Can't open file!\n");

while ($line = <F>) {
    if ($line =~ /$ARGV[0]/) {
        print($line);
    }
}

close(F);
```

Note that you must use =~ for pattern-matching. Other operators – for example, =, ==, or eq – will *not* work.

The regular expression above made use of only concatenation. Let's now consider the other basic operations. First, there is union. Union allows us to stipulate that one or another symbol must occur in some position in the pattern. We use a tiebar | with parentheses to show grouping. For example, to match the pattern abc or adc, we have m/a(b|d)c/.

Essentially, the preceding example puts a union inside a concatenation. We can also put a concatenation inside a union; for example, m/(abc|def)/. This stands for either abc or def.

Finally, we can use Kleene star * to indicate any number of instances of the preceding element (including 0). For example, m/ab*c/ will match ac, abc, abbc, abbbc, and so on. Kleene star can also apply to a union or to a whole string that has been marked with parentheses; for example, m/a(b|c)*d/ or m/a(bc)*d/. The first matches a string composed of an a followed by a d with any number of b's or c's intervening. The second matches a string composed of an a followed by a d with any number of repetitions of bc intervening; for example, ad, abcd, abcbcd, abcbcbcd, and so on.

You can play with these using the two little programs we have written above. However, some of the special characters need to be escaped when entered on the command-line under Windows or Unix. For example, at the DOS prompt, a pattern such as a(b|c)d cannot be entered directly, but must be entered with quotes; for example, perl pat1.pl "a(b|c)d" filename. At the

Unix prompt, union, Kleene star, and parentheses must be preceded by a backslash, and the entire pattern put in double quotes; for example, perl pat1.pl "a\(b\ |c\)d" filename.

6.2   *Special Characters*

Perl regular expressions offer a number of special symbols which are not strictly necessary, but turn out to be quite useful. The most useful are given in the following list:

.   Matches any single character.
^   Matches the beginning of the string.
$ Matches the end of the string.
\w   Matches letters, numbers, and "_".
\W   Matches anything but letters, numbers, and "_".
\s   Matches white space; that is, space, tab, and new line.
\S   Matches anything but white space; that is anything but space and tab.
\d   Matches a number.
\D   Matches anything but a number.
\b   Matches a word boundary.
\B   Matches anything but a word boundary.

Let's look at a few examples to show how these work:

^a.c matches a three-letter sequence at the beginning of the string, where a is the first letter, c is the third, and anything can be the second.
\w$ matches a string that ends with a letter or number.
^\S\S*$ matches a string that has no white space, and that is at least one character long.
\w*\d matches a string composed of any number of letters, numbers, and _ (underscore), but that ends with at least one number.
\b..\b matches two characters at the beginning and end of a word.
\d\d \D\d matches a two-digit number followed by a space, followed by something that isn't a number, and then a single-digit number.

These are actually rather simple; let's consider a few more complex examples:

(ab|(c|de))f   abf or cf or def.
(aa)*b(bb)*   An even number of a's followed by an odd number of b's.
(aa*|b)ab*   Equivalent to aaa*b*|bab* (at least one a followed by any number of b's or ba followed by any number of b's).
((ab)*|(ba)*)   abab... or baba....
(x|y|z)(x|y|z)   xx, xy, xz, yx, yy, yz, zx, zy, zz.

Regular expressions can also be used to define patterns of linguistic interest:

(a|e|i|o|u)   Vowels.
(g|c|t|s|p|w)h   Digraphs with h.
(b|p|m)   Bilabials.
(ed|ing|s|es|t|en)\b   Verbal inflection.
s(i|a|u)ng   Forms of *sing*.
m(ou|s|ic)e   Forms of *mouse*.

Regular expressions can also make use of the characters for tab and new line: \t and \n. For example, to match one or more tabs, this works: /\t\t*/.

We've seen that regular expressions use certain characters in special ways. What if, for example, you wanted to search for a literal asterisk? To use any of the special regular expression characters literally, they must be preceded by a backslash. The following list shows the characters that we have treated so far that must be backslashed in regular expressions:

\(left parenthesis
\)   right parenthesis
*   asterisk
\ | tiebar
\\   backslash

For example, to search for the literal string (a|b), you would use /\(a\ |b\)/.

6.3 *Commenting Regular Expressions*

We've now gotten sufficient machinery that we can create incredibly complex regular expressions. For example: /e(a(ab|c\d*)\W)*d/.[1] Perl provides a convenient mechanism for inserting comments *inside* a regular expression. If the trailing slash of the pattern is suffixed with the letter x, then spaces, tabs, returns, and comments are ignored. This allows us to space out the pieces of a regular expression and insert comments at appropriate intervals. The following simple program demonstrates:

`pat3.pl`

```
open(F, $ARGV[0]) or die("Oops!\n");

while ($line = <F>) {
   if ($line =~
      /e              #begins with e
```

```
        (            #followed by any number of (a(ablc\d*)\W)
     a               #a
        (            #union of (ablc\d*)
           ab  #first conjunct
           |     #or
           c\d*#second conjunct
        )            #end of union
        \W           #nonalphanumeric
     )*              #end of big Kleene group
 d/x                 #ends with a d
 ) {
 print($line);
   }
}

close(F);
```

Comments internal to a regular expression can be quite useful, especially for very large, very complex expressions.

To actually get spaces, tabs, and # in regular expressions with the x flag, they must be backslashed; for example, m/number\ \#3/x.

6.4   *Extra Stuff*

Perl provides other devices that can be used in regular expressions as well. These can be quite convenient for complex expressions. The following list displays them:

[a-f]   The union (disjunction) of the series of items denoted by the hyphenated string – here, all the letters a through f, for example a or b or c or d or e or f.

[xyz]   The union of the letters (equivalent to (xlylz)).

x{m,n}   x must occur at least m times and at most n times.

x+   One or more of x.

x?   Zero or one x.

[^x]   Anything but x.

Here are some examples of these:

[1-5]+   One or more of the integers 1 through 5.

[^aeiou]   Anything but a vowel.

[A-Z]?\d   Zero or one capital letters followed by a single digit.

6.5 *Using Variables in Regular Expressions*

You can perhaps already see how regular expressions can be tailored for language-related purposes. As we've seen, it is a simple matter to define, for example, vowels (/[aeiou]/), verbal inflection (/(edltlinglenls)\b/), and the like.

You can also use variables in regular expressions, which allows you to set up complex regular expressions in a modular fashion. For example, the following program shows how we can define consonants to search for lines of a file that contain final clusters of different sizes:

pat4.pl

```perl
if ($#ARGV != 1) {
   die("Usage:\tperl pat4.pl filename number-of-consonants\n");
}

if ($ARGV[1] =~ /\D/) {
   die("Second argument must be a number\n");
}

$c = "[bcdfghjklmnpqrstvwxz]";
$thepattern = "";

for ($i = 1; $i <= $ARGV[1]; $i++) {
   $thepattern .= $c;
}

$thepattern .= "[\.\?!;: ]";

open(F, $ARGV[0]) or die("Can\'t open file...\n");

while ($line = <F> ) {
   if ($line =~ /$thepattern/) {
      print($line);
   }
}

close(F);
```

First, there are several tests to make sure that the proper number and type of command-line arguments are provided. We then define consonants as a disjunction of consonant letters. The $thepattern variable is initialized to the empty string and these are then appended to the pattern variable as many times as specified by the second argument. (Note that .= is the incrementing concatenation operator, parallel to +=, -=, and so on.) Finally, the consonants must occur at the end of a word, as indicated by various punctuation marks or space.

Perl also provides for several other predefined special variables for use with regular expressions. First, there are the numbered **backreferences**: \1 through \9 and $1 through $9. These allow one to refer back to an element in a regular expression marked with parentheses. The backslash backreferences are used inside the regular expression itself, and the variable backreferences are used outside the pattern up to the next pattern-match. For example, /(.).\1/ matches two identical characters, with a single character intervening; for example, axa, qrq, and so on. Here is an example of a little program that uses both:

back1.pl

```perl
open(F, $ARGV[0]) or die("Oops!\n");

while ($line = <F>) {
   if ($line = /(\w{3,})\1/) {
      print("$1:\t$line");
   }
}

close(F);
```

This program searches a file for sequences of three or more alphanumeric characters that are repeated in sequence; for example, abcabc, xxaxxa, catcat, and so on. If it finds them, it prints out the character sequence that is repeated and the line it occurs in. The regular expression uses \w{3,} to find sequences of at least three characters. That expression is put in parentheses so that it can be backreferenced by \1 later in the pattern, and by $1 later in the program. The \1 detects if the letter sequence is repeated. If so, the if-clause is true, and the consequent applies, printing out the original character sequence with $1, and the entire line as well.

The same construction works if we use the abbreviated if-structure, as in back2.pl below:

back2.pl

```perl
open(F, $ARGV[0]) or die("Oops!\n");

while ($line = <F>) {
   print("$1:\t$line") if ($line =~ /(\w{3,})\1/)
}

close(F);
```

The fact that this works may seem surprising; $1 should refer back to the *previous* pattern-match, yet here there is none. Perl automatically converts the abbreviated if-structure back into its longer form, where the if-test *precedes* the consequent clause. Hence, as far as Perl is concerned, $1 *does* follow the pattern-match in back2.pl.

Finally, Perl pattern-matching defines three special variables: $&, $`, and $'. These are defined by each pattern-match, and refer back, respectively, to the string before the match, the match itself, and the string after the match. Thus, for example, if a string like John loves Mary is matched by /o.*s/, then the three variables will have the following values:

$`	John l
$&	oves
$'	Mary

(Note that $' here has a space as its first character.)

Here is a sample program exemplifying how these special variables can be used:

pat5.pl

```
open(F, $ARGV[1]) or die("Oops!\n");

while ($line = <F>) {
   if ($line =~ /$ARGV[0]/) {
      print("before:\t$`\n");
      print("match:\t$&\n");
      print("after:\t$'\n");
   }
}

close(F);
```

The program takes a filename and pattern as command-line arguments.[2] It then looks for matches line by line, and prints out the match, preceding string, and following string.

6.6   *Greediness*

The regular expression operations that allow for multiple matches are all interpreted "greedily", as matching the largest span possible. For example, if we match the pattern /ab*/ against the string abbbc, the span matched by the pattern ($&) is abbb. Other operations interpreted this way include: +, {,}, and ?.

Perl also allows for "lazy" matching. In this case, the relevant operator is suffixed with ?; for example, *?, +?, ??, and {,}?.[3] In this case, the pattern matches as few instances as possible. Thus, if /ab*?/ is matched against abbbc, it extends only over a. You can test all these combinations by entering appropriate patterns as a command-line argument to pat5.pl.

6.7   *Pig Latin*

The various special variables associated with pattern-matching allow one to manipulate strings directly. Perl actually provides specific tools for this that we treat in the next chapter, but the machinery we've already treated actually allows for quite a bit of power. As an example, we give a simple program in this section for producing language game forms.

The particular language game I use here is **Pig Latin**. The game is played by taking all the consonants at the beginning of a word, moving them to the end, and adding the vowel *ay*, as in *may*, *ray*, *say*, and so on. For example, a word such as *start* is pronounced *art-stay* in Pig Latin.

There are several interesting complications, however. First, what happens with a word that begins with a vowel, such as *ant*? It turns out that there are different dialects of Pig Latin, giving *ant-'ay*, *ant-yay*, or *ant-hay*. The program below models the second dialect, where vowel-initial words get an epenthetic *y*.

The program only handles words that are orthographically vowel-initial, such as *ant*. Words such as *honest* that are phonetically vowel-initial, but begin with an orthographic consonant, are not treated correctly. In the relevant dialect, they are pronounced *onest-yay*, but the program operates from the orthographic representation and produces *onest-hay*.

The other challenge for the program is to treat orthographic *y*, as in words like *myth* and *yacht*. It is a vowel in the first, but a consonant in the second. The program handles this by treating a word-initial *y* followed by a vowel as a consonant. Otherwise, it is treated as a vowel. This handles the two cases above correctly, but also treats words such as *Yvonne* appropriately as well.

The general logic of the program is as follows. The name of a file is given on the command line. There's some error-checking to make sure the number of command-line arguments is appropriate, and then several embedded while-structures. The outermost while-structure loops over each line of the file one by one. The inner while-loop iterates over each word of each line, using backreferences to reset the string each time the pattern match succeeds. Let's go through it line by line.

First, the program checks the number of command-line arguments, defines consonants and vowels, and then opens the file:

piglatin1.pl

```
die("Usage:\tperl piglatin1.pl filename\n") if ($#ARGV != 0);

$c = "[bcdfghjklmnpqrstvwxzBCDFGHJKLMNPQRSTVWXZ]";
$v = "[aeiouyAEIOUY]";

open(F, $ARGV[0]) or die("Oops!\n");
. . .
```

We then come to the first while-loop, the one that iterates over each line of the file. It first checks whether the current line has any characters in it. If it does not, if it is only the return character, then the line is printed:

```
. . .
while ($line = <F>) {
   if (length($line) == 1) {
      print($line);
      . . .
```

If there is more to the line than the return character, then there's a bunch of pattern-matching and reordering. First, we identify the first word on the line with /^(\W*)(\w+)(\W*)/. The parentheses are used so that the individual bits can be manipulated in subsequent code. The idea here is to find the first word on the line, and then use backreferences to reset $line to everything following that first word. Within the current loop, we then process that first word. On each subsequent loop, we process each subsequent word on the line:

```
. . .
} else {
   while ($line =~ /^(\W*)(\w+)(\W*)/) {
      $prebreak = $1;
      $word = $2;
      $break = $3;
      $line = $';
      . . .
```

The rest of the while-loop actually does the Pig Latin changes. The first pattern-match checks for words that begin with *y*, where it is a consonant, *or* for words that begin with a vowel. In either case, the initial *y* is stripped off, and the word is suffixed with *yay*.[4] The second pattern-match handles the general case of words beginning with some number of consonants:

```
        . . .
      if ($word =~ /^[yY]?($v.*)$/) {
          print("$1-yay");
      }elsif ($word =~ /^($c+)(.*)$/) {
          print("$2-$1ay");
      }
      print($break);
   }
 }
}

close(F);
```

This program nicely exemplifies some of the power of backreferences. We will see in the next chapter, however, that Perl provides some dedicated functions for manipulating strings directly without using backreferences.

6.8   *Sentences*

In this section, we develop another program that makes use of regular expressions. This program takes a text file and breaks it up into sentences. The program is interesting for several reasons. First, it makes use of ideas that anticipate machinery introduced in the following chapter. Second, the task is actually rather challenging, although widely applicable in linguistic applications.

The task has several parts. First, we open a file and read through it line by line as usual. We then locate instances of sentence-final punctuation and break each line into fragments based on the punctuation. All the fragments are pushed onto a single array. We then go through the array adding fragments together up to a sentence-final punctuation fragment. Finally, all the sentences are printed out.

Let's now go through the code. The first bit of code assigns a value to $file from the command line and defines sentence-final punctuation. Notice how the latter is perhaps more complicated than expected, because we must accommodate quoted sentences:

sentences.pl

```
$file = $ARGV[0];

#punctuation characters
$punc = "[\.!\?]+[\"']? *";
. . .
```

Next, we open the file and go through it line by line. We remove the final return and check if there is anything left on the line. We define a subroutine below mysplit() that returns a list of the sentence fragments on the line. Each fragment is an instance of $punc or an actual sentence fragment. For example, a line of text such as *and phonemes. Is this a sentence? Yes, it* would be broken up into five fragments: "and phonemes", ". ", "Is this a sentence", "?", and "Yes, it".

```
. . .
open(F, $file) or die("Can't open file.\n");

#split each line into fragments using $punc
while ($line = <F>) {
    chomp($line);
    if (length($line) > 1) {
        push(@fragments, mysplit($line));
    }
}

close(F);
. . .
```

The next loop goes through the fragments once again, appending them together until a sentence-final fragment is reached:

```
. . .
#add all fragments together until an instance of punctuation
for ($i = 1; $i < $#fragments; $i++) {
    if ($fragments[$i-1] !~ /$punc/) {
        $fragments[$i-1] .= $fragments[$i];
        splice(@fragments, $i, 1);
        $i--;
    }
}
. . .
```

Each fragment is now a sentence and is printed out:

```
. . .
#print out each sentence
for ($i = 0; $i < $#fragments; $i++) {
    print("$fragments[$i]\n\n");
}
. . .
```

The mysplit() subroutine appears at the end of the program. The core of the method is a while-structure that checks the line for instances of $punc. If it finds one, it pushes the preceding string and the match onto @frags. It then tries again with everything after the match. This procedure works because the pattern matches the first instance of $punc in the line. Finally, the contents of @frags are returned:

```
. . .
#splits the line repeatedly into fragments
sub mysplit {
    my(@frags, $line);
    $line = shift();
    while ($line =~ /$punc/) {
        push(@frags,$`);
        push(@frags,$&);
        $line = $';
    }
    push(@frags,$line);
    return(@frags);
}
```

6.9   *Summary*

This chapter has introduced one of the most important and powerful aspects of Perl: pattern-matching and regular expressions. Pattern-matching allows one to inspect any sort of input for string patterns. Regular expression syntax provides for an extremely versatile range of patterns.

Formally, Perl regular expressions can be (virtually!) reduced to three simple operations: concatenation, union, and Kleene star. In practice, however, Perl provides for many abbreviatory conventions to characterize string patterns. These include a number of special constructions, but also many special variables for various classes of characters.

Perl also provides, via the m//x construction, for embedded comments in regular expressions. Thus, although interesting regular expressions can quickly become quite complex, it is possible to document a pattern exhaustively.

Finally, Perl also allows for variables in pattern-matching. There are two ways of backreferencing available: both internal to the pattern being matched, and after the last pattern matched. These allow one to manipulate strings in very intricate ways. We will see some additional tools for this in the next chapter.

6.10 Exercises

1. For your operating system, show precisely which special regular expression operators cannot be entered directly on the command line and how they must be escaped (backslashed) so that they will work.
2. Revise the piglatin1.pl program so that it produces one of the other Pig Latin dialects instead.
3. Regular expression exercises:
   (a) Give three ways of matching all vowels except i.
   (b) What does this abbreviate: /\\\\a/?
   (c) Given a file composed of a single column of words, give a regular expression that will find all two-syllable words.
   (d) Given the same type of file, give a regular expression that will match any word that does not contain two identical letters in a row.
   (e) What does this abbreviate: / \$ $ /x?
   (f) Write a regular expression to match any word containing an even number of vowels.
4. The mysplit() function can be mirrored by a function that does the reverse. This new function takes two arguments: a string and a list. It returns a string where all the elements of the list are joined by instances of the string; for example, myjoin("-",('a','b','c')) produces a-b-c. Write this function as a separate module.

Notes

[1] This matches edeaab d, eac7 d, and so on.
[2] Don't forget that patterns entered on the command line need to be escaped properly under Unix or Windows.
[3] Question mark thus has two interpretations in regular expressions: "zero or one" or laziness.
[4] Notice that the other Pig Latin dialects would be somewhat more difficult to treat! This is left as an exercise.

Chapter 7

Text Manipulation

In this chapter, we augment our pattern-matching toolbox. We present several functions for manipulating strings: s/// and tr///. The former is used for string replacement and the latter for character-by-character replacement.

In addition, we treat the split() and join() functions, which are used to split a string into tokens, or join a list of strings into a bigger string.

Finally, we introduce **hash**es, an extremely important data structure. We use these devices to develop a concordancing program and to develop a program for collecting letter bigrams.

7.1   s///

The s/// function is actually not required formally, but is quite convenient nonetheless. It allows one to replace some string by some other string. For example, something like $string =˜ s/hat/box/; replaces the first instance of hat with box in $string. Like m//, s/// is bound to the string with =˜, *not* with == or =.

If s/// is used with the g flag ("global") which replaces *all* instances of the pattern in the string in question, then using s/// with = returns the number of matches. Using it with =˜ replaces all instances of the pattern.

Here is a simple program that takes the two arguments for s/// and a filename from the command line. It prints out each line in the file after all replacements have been made. It also keeps track of the number of replacements made. It uses the g flag to force all possible replacements on each line.

replace1.pl

```
open(F, $ARGV[2]) or die("Oops!\n");

while ($line = <F>) {
    $num += ($line =~ s/$ARGV[0]/$ARGV[1]/g);
    print($line);
}

close(F);

print("how many:\t$num\n");
```

The substitutions are stored in $line, while $num keeps track of the number of substitutions made. Without the g flag, $num would only keep track of the number of lines that contain the pattern, incrementing only once even for lines that contain more than one instance of the pattern.

Interestingly, m//g can be used to simply test for how many times a pattern occurs, but the number of matches isn't returned the same way. The following program keeps track of the number of times a pattern is matched in a file. The program also keeps track of the maximum number of matches per line.

pat6.pl

```
open(F, $ARGV[1]) or die("Oops!\n");

$biggest = 0;

while ($line = <F>) {
    $lines++;
    $matches = 0;
    $matches++ while ($line =~ /$ARGV[0]/g);
    $allmatches += $matches;
    $biggest = $matches if ($matches > $biggest);
}

close(F);

print("Total number of lines:\t$lines\n");
print("Total matches:\t$allmatches\n");
print("Max per line:\t$biggest\n");
```

Here $lines keeps track of the number of lines in the file. The $matches variable is reset to zero every time a line is read from the file and keeps track of the number of matches in the current line. It does this with a while-structure iterating over the number of matches with m//g. The total number of matches is kept in $allmatches, and the largest number of matches in any line is stored in $biggest. Finally, the results are printed to the screen.

The substitution function takes a number of other flags as well. The most important are s///x and s///e. The former is just like m//x, allowing the programmer to interpose spaces and comments for clarity.

The s///e flag ("expression"), however, is quite interesting; it forces Perl to interpret the second argument to s///e as a full Perl expression. Here is a very simple example:

`replace2.pl`

```
open(F, $ARGV[0]) or die("Oops!\n");

while ($line = <F>) {
    $line =~ s/
        \d+ #some number of digits
        /
        $& #the numbers again
        *3 #multiplied by 3
        /gxe;
    print($line);
}

close(F);
```

The substitution is given three flags. The g flag allows for multiple substitutions on the same line. The x flag allows for the interspersed spaces and comments. Finally, the e flag allows the second argument of s/// to be interpreted as a Perl expression. Here, that argument is $& * 3; this multiplies the number found by the pattern-matcher by three, replacing the original number by this product.

The e flag even allows you to insert your own subroutines as a second argument. The following program does exactly the same thing as the preceding one:

`replace3.pl`

```
open(F, $ARGV[0]) or die("Oops!\n");

while ($line = <F>) {
    $line =~ s/\d+/times3($&)/ge;
    print($line);
}
```

```
close(F);

sub times3 {
    my $in = shift();
    return($in * 3);
}
```

7.2   tr///

The tr/// function is for making character-by-character substitutions. It takes two arguments, each of which is a list of characters. The lists can also be given as sequences; for example, a-z or 1-9. Here is a simple program for replacing each digit with the corresponding letter of the alphabet:

replace4.pl

```
open(F, $ARGV[0]) or die("Oops!\n");

while ($line = <F>) {
    $line =~ tr/0-9/a-j/;
    print($line);
}

close(F);
```

Note that by its very nature, the tr/// command does not use a g flag. It always applies in a "global" fashion, making all possible replacements.

Here is a more useful example of tr///. The following program takes all vowels with an acute accent, á, é, í, ó, and ú, and replaces them with unaccented vowels:

replace5.pl

```
open(F, $ARGV[0]) or die("Oops!\n");

while ($line = <F>) {
    $line =~ tr/\341\351\355\363\372/aeiou/;
    print($line);
}

close(F);
```

Perl regular expressions can refer to characters by their octal numbers.[1] The appropriate octal number is preceded by a backslash. Thus \341 is á.

Here is a little Perl module for retrieving octal numbers from characters:

Octal.pm

```
package Octal;

use Exporter;
@ISA = ("Exporter");
@EXPORT = ("char2octal");

sub char2octal {
    my($arg) = shift();
    $arg = ord($arg);
    $arg = sprintf("%o", $arg);
    return($arg);
}

1;
```

The program begins with the package declaration and ends with the true statement required by all Perl modules. Next, there are the three lines that allow programs calling the module to use simply the subroutine name in each invocation.

The module defines a single subroutine char2octal(). It first takes a single argument from @_, and applies the ord() function to it, retrieving its ASCII number. That number is then converted to octal using the sprintf() function. Finally, char2octal() returns the number determined.

The tr/// command would seem to require that the length of its two lists be the same, but this is not the case. If the second argument is longer than the first, extra characters are ignored. For example, tr/abc/1234/ would convert a to 1, b to 2, and c to 3, ignoring 4. On the other hand, if the second argument is shorter than the first, then extra items in the first argument are translated as the last item of the second argument. For example, tr/abc/12/ would convert a to 1, b to 2, and c to 2.

If, however, tr/// is used with the d flag ("delete"), then unpaired items from the first argument are deleted. For example, tr/abc/12/d would convert a to 1, b to 2, and delete c, rather than converting it to 2.

Here is a little program that simply deletes numbers:

replace6.pl

```
open(F, $ARGV[0]) or die("Oops!\n");

while ($line = <F>) {
    $line =~ tr/0-9//d;
    print($line);
}

close(F);
```

Finally, tr/// behaves like s/// in that it returns the number of matches when used with =. The following simple program, which counts digits, exemplifies:

replace7.pl

```
open(F, $ARGV[0]) or die("Oops!\n");

while ($line = <F>) {
    $num += $line =~ tr/0-9/0-9/;
}

close(F);

print("$num\n");
```

7.3   split() *and* join()

The split() function is an *extremely* useful one. It takes two arguments, the first of which is a pattern while the second is a string. What split() does is break a string up into tokens at every occurrence of the pattern. The result of split() is a list of tokens. For example, @words = split(/ /, $string); would split the string $string up into individual tokens, at each space, and put the results into the array @words.

The split() function is most useful for finding the words in a file for subsequent processing. Here is a simple example, where split() is used to find all the sentences in a file, each of which is printed out separately. (Over the next few programs, we develop a revision of the sentences.pl program from the previous chapter.)

split1.pl

```
open(F, $ARGV[0]) or die("Oops!\n");

while ($line = <F>) {
   @f = split(/[\.\?!]/, $line);
   push(@frags, @f);
}

close(F);

foreach $frag (@frags) {
   if ($frag =~ /\n$/) {
      chomp($frag);
      print("$frag ");
   } else {
      print("$frag\n\n");
   }
}
```

The program takes a filename from the command line. It goes through the file line by line, splitting the line into fragments at each occurrence of a sentence punctuation mark. These sentence fragments are then pushed onto a big array of fragments. Finally, the fragments are printed out one by one. If the current fragment ends in a return, then it must be a sentence that wraps across two lines. In these cases, the return is replaced with a space. If, on the other hand, the fragment does not end in a return, then it must be a sentence-final fragment, in which case it is printed, followed by several returns to separate it from the next sentence.

One problem with this program is that it loses what the particular punctuation was that terminated the sentence. This can be rectified by putting parentheses in the pattern used to split the line into fragments. If the pattern used by split() is marked with parentheses, then split() will return the delimiters, as well as the fragments, in the array. The following revision does this:

split2.pl

```
open(F, $ARGV[0]) or die("Oops!\n");

while ($line = <F>) {
   @f = split(/([\.\?!])/, $line);
   push(@frags, @f);
}
```

```
close(F);

foreach $frag (@frags) {
   if ($frag !~ /\w/) {
      print("$frag\n\n");
   } else {
      print("$frag");
   }
}
```

Here the foreach loop first tests if the current fragment is a punctuation mark. If it is, it prints it followed by several returns. If it is not, it just prints the fragment. Notice how the parentheses in the invocation of split() return the punctuation that the foreach loop tests for.

There are several problems still with this version of the program. The main one is that it doesn't save the sentences into any kind of usable data structure. That is, if we want to actually do something with the sentences we are locating in the file, this program won't allow for it. There is another problem as well: the current program doesn't handle line breaks very well. It would be useful to strip line breaks and replace them with spaces. It will turn out that this is much easier once we've actually saved each sentence separately. The following revision handles these:

split3.pl

```
open(F, $ARGV[0]) or die("Oops!\n");

$punc = "[\.\?!]";

while ($line = <F>) {
   @f = split(/($punc)/, $line);
   push(@frags, @f);
}

close(F);

foreach $frag (@frags) {
   $sentence .= $frag;
   if ($frag =~ /$punc/) {
      $sentence =~ tr/\n/ /;
      $sentence =~ s/ +/ /g;
      $sentence =~ s/^\W+//;
```

```
        push(@sentences, $sentence);
        $sentence = "";
    }
}

foreach $s (@sentences) {
    print("$s\n\n");
}
```

First, we put the punctuation characters in a variable, since we will be referring to them more than once.[2] Next, we go through the file, line by line as
before, breaking it into fragments based on sentence punctuation. As before,
this results in three sorts of fragments: (i) fragments terminated by a line
break, (ii) fragments preceding sentence punctuation, and (iii) the sentence
punctuation itself. Finally, the program loops through the fragments, reas-
sembling them into sentence-sized units. Each fragment is concatenated to
the current sentence. If the fragment is a sentence punctuation character, then
the current sentence is complete and added to an array of sentences. Before
being added to the array, returns are replaced by spaces, and extra spaces are
removed.

As one might expect, split() is mirrored by another function for joining
strings together: join(). The join() function takes a string and a list as arguments. The string is what is used as "glue" to tie the elements of the list into
a single string. For example, the statement print(join("-", 1..5)) prints out 1-
2-3-4-5.

7.4   *The Anonymous Variable Again*

We have covered all of the following pattern-matching functions:

m//   Matches a pattern.
tr///   Makes character-by-character substitutions/translations.
s///   Does string substitution(s).
split(//, string)   Splits a string up based on a delimiter specified as a regular
   expression.

All of the pattern-matching functions can be used with the anonymous
variable. As usual, this can be confusing, but it is done quite often and can be
quite convenient. The split3.pl program above made use of all of them. The
following program revises split3.pl to make use of the anonymous variable
whenever possible:

split4.pl

```perl
open(F, $ARGV[0]) or die("Oops!\n");

$punc = "[\.\?!]";

while (<F>) {
    @f = split(/($punc)/);
    push(@frags, @f);
}

close(F);

foreach (@frags) {
    $sentence .= $_;
    if (/$punc/) {
        $sentence =~ tr/\n/ /;
        $sentence =~ s/ +/ /g;
        $sentence =~ s/^\W+//;
        push(@sentences, $sentence);
        $sentence = "";
    }
}

foreach (@sentences) {
    print();
    print("\n\n");
}
```

This program shows how m// and split() can be used with the anonymous variable.

The following simple program shows how tr/// and s/// can also be used with it. The program is a silly one. It replaces every instance of the word "fruit" with "vegetable", and capitalizes all vowels.

anon1.pl

```perl
open(F, $ARGV[0]) or die("Oops!\n");

while (<F>) {
    s/[Ff]ruit/vegetable/g;
    tr/aeiou/AEIOU/;
```

```
   print();
}
```

```
close(F);
```

Finally, note how m// can occur with the anonymous variable with while if the g flag is used. The following program prints out all capitalized words in a file:

anon2.pl

```
open(F, $ARGV[0]) or die("Oops!\n");

while (<F>) {
   while (/[A-Z]\w*/g) {
      print("$&\n");
   }
}

close(F);
```

This program is quite interesting, because the anonymous variable is used *twice*. There is an outer while-loop where on each iteration, $_ is set to the current line of the file. Then there is an inner while-loop that iterates over matches in the line.

7.5   sort()

The sort() function takes a list argument and returns a sorted list. It also allows you to specify – with an optional first argument – a specific comparison method. For example, sort('d', 'a', 'b'); returns the list ('a', 'b', 'd'). Here is a simple program that takes a filename argument on the command line, and prints out a sorted list of the words in that file:

sort1.pl

```
open(F, $ARGV[0]) or die("Uh-oh!\n");

while ($line = <F>) {
   @wordsInLine = split(/\W+/, $line);
   push(@words, @wordsInLine);
}
```

```
close(F);

foreach $word (sort(@words)) {
   print("$word\n");
}
```

Everything here is as usual, except the invocation of sort() in the foreach structure. Here, sort() allows foreach to return the items of @words in sorted order.

The default sort order is that returned by the built-in cmp operator. This returns -1, 0, or 1, depending on whether its first operand is less than, equal to, or greater than the second operand alphabetically. Note that capital letters are less than lower-case letters.

This can be changed by invoking sort() with an explicit sorting function as a first argument. This function can either be laid out explicitly as the first argument, or defined by a subroutine name, given elsewhere in the program. There are two things to keep in mind about this sorting function, however. First, like cmp, your sorting function must return -1, 0, or 1, depending on the relationship between the sorted elements. Second, the sorting function should not take explicit arguments, but should use the global predefined variables $a and $b.[3] The sort() function automatically places the elements to be compared in these variables. The following program shows how a sorting function can be provided:

sort2.pl

```
open(F, $ARGV[0]) or die("Uh-oh!\n");

while ($line = <F>) {
   @wordsInLine = split(/\W+/, $line);
   push(@words, @wordsInLine);
}

close(F);

print("sorted with default sorting routine:\n");

foreach $word (sort(@words)) {
   print("$word\n");
}

print("Sorted with specified sorting routine:\n");
```

```
foreach $word (sort({$a cmp $b} @words)) {
    print("$word\n");
}

print("Sorted with subroutine:\n");

foreach $word (sort(boring @words)) {
    print("$word\n");
}

sub boring {
    return($a cmp $b);
}
```

In the above program, the words to be sorted are taken from a file given on the command line. As in the previous program, the lines are broken up into words and put in an array which is then sorted. Here that array is sorted three times. Here, each sort is exactly the same. The first invocation of sort() uses the default alphabetic sorting routine. The second invocation does exactly the same thing, by specifying that scheme as the first argument to sort(). Notice that the arguments are *not* separated with a comma, as with print() (when used with a handle). Finally, the third sort does the same thing again, in a different way, by putting the sorting routine in a separate subroutine which is invoked by name as the first argument of sort().

Specifying a sorting routine can have far more useful consequences. For example, items can be sorted in reverse alphabetical order by specifying the sorting routine as {$b cmp $a}. Sorting in a case-insensitive fashion can be done with the built-in functions lc() and uc() which return the lower-case or upper-case versions of their arguments respectively. For example, {lc($a) cmp lc($b)} results in a case-insensitive alphabetic sort. Finally, a numerical sort can be obtained by using the numerical comparison operator <=>. Thus, {$a <=> $b} gives a numerical comparison.

Here is a final example of using sort(). The following program collects the words of a file and then sorts them by length. However, upper-case words all precede lower-case words:

`sort3.pl`

```
open(F, $ARGV[0]) or die("Uh-oh!\n");

while ($line = <F>) {
    @wordsInLine = split(/\W+/, $line);
    push(@words, @wordsInLine);
}
```

```
close(F);

foreach $word (sort(mysort @words)) {
    print("$word\n");
}

sub mysort {
    if ($a =~ /^[A-Z]/ and $b =~ /^[A-Z]/) {
        return(length($a) <=> length($b));
    } elsif ($a !~ /^[A-Z]/ and $b !~ /^[A-Z]/) {
        return(length($a) <=> length($b));
    } elsif ($a =~ /^[A-Z]/) {
        return(-1);
    } else {
        return(1);
    }
}
```

The sorting routine is relatively straightforward. If both words begin with an upper-case letter, they are sorted by length. If both begin with a lower-case letter, they are sorted by length. Else, the word that begins with an upper-case letter goes first.

7.6 *Hashes*

Using split() to break lines into words and store them in arrays results in repeated tokens if words are repeated in a file. Perl provides a very convenient data structure which we can use to avoid this: a **hash**. A hash – or hashtable – is very much like an array. Like an array, it is a set of variables linked together. However, it is unlike an array in two respects. First, unlike an array, the elements of a hash have no particular order; they are a set, rather than a list. Second, unlike an array, the elements of a hash are *named*, rather than indexed.

The syntax for hashes is different from arrays. An entire hash is denoted with a leading %, e.g. %myhash. Individual hash elements are denoted with a leading $, just like individual array elements, but with curly braces around the name, rather than square braces; for example, $myhash{aname}. Note that the individual hash element name does *not* need to be quoted. Thus $myhash{'aname'} is the same thing as $myhash{aname}. Individual hash names are called **keys** and the contents of individual hash elements are called **values**.

Here is a very simple example showing how hashes can be used. The program creates a hash called %myhash. The user can call individual hash element keys on the command line, and the program prints out the appropriate value:

`hash1.pl`

```
$myhash{lion} = 6;
$myhash{tiger} = "lion";
$myhash{bear} = $myhash{lion} . " " . $myhash{tiger} . "s";

print($myhash{$ARGV[0]} . "\n");
```

The names and values given here are meant to help distinguish the keys from the values. For example, $myhash{tiger} has a value lion, but a key tiger. On the other hand, the element $myhash{lion} has a key lion, but a value 6. Thus, if the user enters lion on the command line, the program prints out "6". If the user enters tiger on the command line, the program prints out "lion", and if the user enters bear, then the program prints out "6 lions". Remember that the easiest way to think of a hash is like an array, but where the individual elements are *named*, rather than *numbered*.

Notice too how the array element $ARGV[0] can be used as the key of %myhash. In this case, the string contained in $ARGV[0] is used as the name/key of %myhash.

We now have enough funny symbols for Perl data types that it is convenient to review them:[4]

$a	variable
%a	hash
@a	array
$a{name}	hash element
$a[1]	array element
A	filehandle

There are a number of functions that are used with hashes, and I will go through each of them now.

7.6.1   exists()

The exists() function returns true if its argument actually exists. It is particularly useful for checking if some particular hash-key combination is actually defined. For example, we can add a clause to the program above to check whether the command-line argument entered by the user is actually an existing key of %myhash:

hash2.pl

```
$myhash{lion} = 6;
$myhash{tiger} = "lion";
$myhash{bear} = $myhash{lion} . " " . $myhash{tiger} . "s";
if (exists($myhash{$ARGV[0]})) {
   print($myhash{$ARGV[0]} . "\n");
} else {
   print("Not a key in this hash!\n");
}
```

Note that if no argument is entered on the command line, the program treats that as an instance of a nonexisting hash key.

7.6.2   delete()

Another very useful function for hashes is delete(), which removes a hash element. The following program exemplifies. First, like the previous programs exemplifying hashes, it creates a hash with several named elements. It then goes into a loop, prompting the user to enter new hash elements. If the user enters an existing hash key, it is deleted; if the user enters a nonexisting hash key, it is added.

hash3.pl

```
$myhash{lion} = 6;
$myhash{tiger} = "lion";
$myhash{bear} = $myhash{lion} . " " . $myhash{tiger} . "s";
enter();

while (length($line) > 0) {
   if (exists($myhash{$line})) {
      print("The value of \$myhash{$line} was: $myhash{$line}\n");
      delete($myhash{$line});
   } else {
      print("New key!\nEnter a value: ");
      $val = <STDIN>;
      chomp($val);
      $myhash{$line} = $val;
   }
   enter();
}
```

```
sub enter {
   print("Enter a key: ");
   $line = <STDIN>;
   chomp($line);
}
```

There are three parts to the program. The first part initializes the hash as usual, with the same key–value pairs as the preceding programs. The second part of the program is a subroutine called enter(), which collects input from the user, puts it in a variable $line, and chomps off the terminating return.

The main part of the program is a while-loop, which iterates as long as the user entered something to the enter() subroutine. Within the while-loop, there is an if-test, which checks if what the user entered is a valid key in $myhash. If it is, its value is printed out and it is removed from the hash with delete(). If it is not, then the user is prompted for a value, and the new key–value pair is added to the hash.

Note especially the first print() statement in the if-structure, informing the user of the current value of the key entered. Notice how the backslash is used so that the literal string $myhash{ . . . } can be represented in the first part of the string. There's nothing especially new here, but it shows once again how when using Perl, one must attend to the niceties of putting backslashes in the right places.

7.6.3   keys()

Perl also offers a function keys() which is extremely useful for iterating through the keys of a hash. What it does is return all the keys of a hash as a list. Thus keys(%myhash) returns a list of all the keys in %myhash. Let's exemplify this by revising the hash3.pl program above. This program prints out the contents of the hash before prompting the user to enter a key. It responds to that key just like the preceding program:

hash4.pl

```
$myhash{lion} = 6;
$myhash{tiger} = "lion";
$myhash{bear} = $myhash{lion} . " " . $myhash{tiger} . "s";

enter();

while (length($line) > 0) {
   if (exists($myhash{$line})) {
      delete($myhash{$line});
   } else {
```

```
        print("New key!\nEnter a value: ");
        $val = <STDIN>;
        chomp($val);
        $myhash{$line} = $val;
    }
    enter();
}

sub enter {
    printall();
    print("Enter a key: ");
    $line = <STDIN>;
    chomp($line);
}

sub printall {
    foreach $key (keys(%myhash)) {
        print("$key\t$myhash{$key}\n");
    }
}
```

The program adds a new subroutine printall() which prints out each key–value pair in the array. It does this by using keys() to return a list of keys, and foreach to step through that list assigning each key to the variable $key.

It is extremely important to note that keys are returned *in no specific order*. It is neither alphabetical or chronological. Rather, the order depends on Perl's internal treatment of hashes. However, if you do want to examine the keys in a specific order, it is a simple matter to prefix the keys() command with the sort() command. The following program simply adds in a case-insensitive sorting of the keys:

hash5.pl

```
$myhash{lion} = 6;
$myhash{tiger} = "lion";
$myhash{bear} = $myhash{lion} . " " . $myhash{tiger} . "s";
enter();

while (length($line) > 0) {
    if (exists($myhash{$line})) {
        delete($myhash{$line});
    } else {
        print("New key!\nEnter a value: ");
        $val = <STDIN>;
```

```
        chomp($val);
        $myhash{$line} = $val;
    }
    enter();
}

sub enter {
    printall();
    print("Enter a key: ");
    $line = <STDIN>;
    chomp($line);
}

sub printall {
    foreach $key (sort({lc($a) cmp lc($b)} keys(%myhash))) {
        print("$key\t$myhash{$key}\n");
    }
}
```

The only addition here is sort {lc($a) cmp lc($b)} before the keys() command.

7.6.4   values()

Perl also offers a command for stepping through the values of a hash, but it is far less useful. In its bare form, values() can always be replaced with a call to keys() and then using the respective key to access the relevant value. The following program exemplifies:

hash6.pl

```
$myhash{lion} = 6;
$myhash{tiger} = "lion";
$myhash{bear} = $myhash{lion} . " " . $myhash{tiger} . "s";

print("using \"values\"\n");
foreach $val (values(%myhash)) {
    print("value:\t$val\n");
}

print("\nusing \"keys\"\n");
foreach $key (keys(%myhash)) {
    print("value:\t$myhash{$key}\n");
}
```

However, if you wish to return a *sorted* list of the values in a hash, then values() is quite convenient. The following program shows how this is done, and it also shows how it can be done less conveniently using keys():

hash7.pl

```
$myhash{lion} = 6;
$myhash{tiger} = "lion";
$myhash{bear} = $myhash{lion} . " " . $myhash{tiger} . "s";

print("using \"values\"\n");
foreach $val (sort(values(%myhash))) {
    print("value:\t$val\n");
}

print("\nusing \"keys\"\n");
foreach $key (keys(%myhash)) {
    push(@myarray, $myhash{$key});
}
foreach $index (sort(@myarray)) {
    print("value:\t$index\n");
}
```

As before, the hash is initialized at the beginning of the program. The next few lines add sort() to the code for stepping through the values of a hash. Finally, the last few lines show how the values of a hash can be sorted without recourse to values(). First, you can use keys() to access the values of the hash, pushing each value onto a new temporary array. You then use foreach and sort() to print out the values in sorted order. Notice, incidentally, that this program demonstrates that sort() can also be used with array elements.

7.6.5   each()

Finally, Perl offers a final command that returns entire key–value pairs: each(). The following program exemplifies:

hash8.pl

```
$myhash{lion} = 6;
$myhash{tiger} = "lion";
$myhash{bear} = $myhash{lion} . " " . $myhash{tiger} . "s";
```

```
while (($key, $value) = each(%myhash)) {
    print("$key:\t$value\n");
}
```

Here, we step through the elements returned by each() with a while-structure. Since each() returns a *list* of elements, we enclose our variables in parentheses. Moreover, we cannot use foreach with each() because foreach only works with singleton elements, rather than lists.

The each() command is of limited utility, but we include it for completeness.

7.7   Concordances

This chapter has introduced some of the essential tools that Perl offers for text manipulation. In this section, we use these to develop several programs for building **concordances** of various types. A concordance is a list of the words that occur in a text. With the tools from this chapter, we can construct concordances quite easily.

Here's a very simple program that simply counts the occurrences of words in a file:

conc1.pl

```
open(F, $ARGV[0]) or die("Enter a file name\n");

while ($line = <F>) {
    chomp($line);
    @words = split(/[ \.\?,!;:]+/, $line);
    foreach $word (@words) {
        $conc{$word}++;
    }
}

close(F);

foreach $word (sort(keys(%conc))) {
    print("$word:\t$conc{$word}\n");
}
```

The program takes a filename as a command-line argument. There is then a while-loop to read the file line by line. Each line is split up into words and the words are added to an array. The words in the array are then added to a hash %conc one by one. (Recall the way ++ works with uninitialized variables in a numerical context: it sets the initial value to 0.) If the hash key is new, it is assigned the value of 1. If the key already exists in the hash, its value is augmented by one.

This concordance is only partially successful. There are two obvious flaws. First, it counts capitalized instances of a word separately from lower-case instances. Second, it sorts these separately. The following revision addresses these problems, by converting all words to lower case before adding them to the array:

conc2.pl

```perl
open(F, $ARGV[0]) or die("Enter a file name\n");

while ($line = <F>) {
    chomp($line);
    @words = split(/[ \.\?,!;:]+/, $line);
    foreach $word (@words) {
        $word = lc($word);
        $conc{$word}++;
    }
}

close(F);

foreach $word (sort(keys(%conc))) {
    print("$word:\t$conc{$word}\n");
}
```

While this would seem to solve the problem, it does so by obliterating the difference between capitalized and lower-case letters in *all* locations. Thus, when a word such as "John" occurs in the middle of a sentence, we want to preserve the capitalization, and our program loses this.

Let's now write a program that keeps track of the correct capitalization of a word. The rules of capitalization in English would seem straightforward. All words are capitalized at the beginning of a sentence; proper nouns are capitalized everywhere.

First, the program must distinguish between sentence-initial words and all other words. If a word is capitalized in medial position, then it is a proper noun and its capitalization is preserved. The program must also have an algorithm for dealing with sentence-initial words. This, in fact, is a rather complex problem. Let's have the program solve it by comparing sentence-initial words to medial words. For example, if the program finds sentence-initial "Hats", and finds medial "hats", but not medial "Hats", it will convert "Hats" to lower case and thus treat it as a normal noun. If the program finds sentence-initial "Hortence", and finds medial "Hortence", but no medial "hortence", then it will treat the sentence-initial word as a proper noun. This will work in the general case, but can fail just in case the text is skewed in the following way. Imagine, for example, that the text contains the proper noun "John", but only in sentence-initial position. On the other hand, for some reason, all the sentence-medial occurrences are of the common noun "john" (which has several other meanings). In such a case, the algorithm would fail. I leave this possibility aside.

There is another possibility as well. Imagine that a text contains medial instances of "John" *and* "john". What should the algorithm do then? The following program treats such cases as proper nouns. The assumption is that it would be exceedingly unlikely for a common noun such as "john" to occur sentence-initially.

Let's go through the program slowly and see how it works. First, the program is invoked with a command-line argument which gives the name of the file to be concordanced. The program first opens this file. Next, the program sets the value of a flag that it uses to keep track of whether the current word is at the beginning of a sentence or not. The logic is that words and punctuation will be read from the file one by one. If a sentence-final punctuation mark is read, the flag is set to 1, or true. Once the program has processed a sentence-initial word, the flag is set back to 0, or false:

conc3.pl

```
open(F, $ARGV[0]) or die("Enter a file name\n");

$initial = 1;
. . .
```

The next bit of the program is a large while-structure for iterating over the lines of the file. Each line is read, the final return is stripped off, and then it is split up into words:

```
. . .
while ($line = <F>) {
    chomp($line);
    @words = split(/([ \.\?,!;:]+)/, $line);
    . . .
```

Notice how the characters that are fed to split() for separating words are put into parentheses. Recall that parentheses here force split() to return not just the tokens, but the separating characters in the list. We will use these characters to set the $initial flag.

The next part of the program is a large foreach structure for iterating through the words (and punctuation!) returned by split(). The basic idea here is to monitor the current token for whether or not it is an instance of sentence-final punctuation. This is used to set $initial. At the same time, the value of $initial is monitored. There are four basic cases to consider, separated here at the highest level into four separate if/elsif/else blocks. The first checks if the current word is sentence-final punctuation. If so, it sets the $initial flag to true. The second clause checks if the current word is some other sort of word-separating punctuation. If so, nothing happens. The third clause handles a sentence-initial word, and the fourth clause handles a sentence-medial word. In both cases, the words are added to a hash and the number of occurrences is summed:

```
. . .
foreach $word (@words) {
    if ($word =~ /[\.\?!]+/) {
        $initial = 1;
    } elsif ($word =~ /[ ;:]+/) {
        #do nothing in this case!
    } elsif ($initial) {
        $initial = 0;
        $init{$word}++;
    } else {
        $medial{$word}++;
    }
}
}

close(F);
. . .
```

The next bit of code collapses the two hashes according to the algorithm given above. It iterates over all the words in the hash of sentence-initial words. It creates a lower-case copy and then checks the sentence-medial hash for whether the word – or lower-case copy – exists. Finally, the merged hash is printed out after being sorted in a case-insensitive fashion:

```
. . .
foreach $initword (keys(%init)) {
    $lcword = lc($initword);
    if (exists $medial{$initword}) {
        $medial{$initword} += $init{$initword};
    } elsif (exists $medial{$lcword}) {
```

```
      $medial{$lcword} += $init{$initword};
    } else {
      $medial{$initword} = $init{$initword};
    }
}

foreach $word (sort({lc($a) cmp lc($b)} keys(%medial))) {
    print("$word:\t$medial{$word}\n");
}
```

7.8   Bigrams

In this section, we develop a program for collecting two-letter sequences, or
bigrams. This is a very similar task to concordancing and we make use of
similar techniques.

A text can be conceived as a sequence of elements: letters/sounds, words,
sentences, and so on. In computational linguistics, bigram distributions can
be used to model a text (or language). It is therefore necessary to collect
frequency information about bigrams to construct these models.

The program below collects bigram frequency information for within-word
bigrams. The logic of the program is as follows. We collect the name of the
file on the command line. We then loop through the file line by line, using
chomp() to strip the line-final return. Within this loop, we use split() to separate the line into individual words, and then use foreach to consider each
word in the line. Within this embedded loop, we then iterate across each
word using substr(). This function takes three arguments and returns a
substring of its string argument. The first argument is a string. The second is
an index for where the substring begins. The third is an integer that represents the length of the substring. We can use substr() to extract the bigrams of
each word. We use a hash to keep track of the frequency of each bigram.
Finally, we print out each bigram and its frequency:

bigrams.pl

```
open(F, $ARGV[0]) or die("Can't open file!\n");

while ($line = <F>) {
    chomp($line);
    @words = split(/\W+/, $line);
    foreach $word (@words) {
        $wordlength = length($word);
        if ($wordlength > 1) {
            for ($i = 0; $i < $wordlength - 1; $i++) {
```

```
            $bigram = substr($word,$i,2);
            $bigrams{$bigram}++;
        }
    }
  }
}

close(F);

foreach $bigram (sort(keys(%bigrams))) {
    print("$bigram\t$bigrams{$bigram}\n");
}
```

7.9 Summary

This chapter has introduced some of the most important Perl functions and structures for manipulating text.

First, we introduced the commands for string replacement, either on the string level or on the character level. The s/// command is used for string substitution and the tr/// command is used for character substitution.

We also introduced the split() and join() commands which allow us to break a string up into word- or sentence-like tokens, and assemble the same.

Third, we went over the sort() command which provides for any type of sort.

Most importantly, we introduced **hash**es, a data structure that is extremely useful for text manipulation. Hashes are like arrays in that they represent a group of related variables. However, hashes provide a "name", rather than an index for its group of variables. Thus hashes define a set of named variables.

We also covered a number of commands that are quite useful with hashes; for example, keys(), values(), exists(), and delete().

Finally, we concluded the chapter with several programs for making concordances from text files.

7.10 Exercises

1. Rewrite the replace1.pl program on page 95 using backreferences instead of s///.
2. The replace6.pl program on page 99 can be rewritten in at least *two* other ways. Do so.

3. The concordance program we wrote in the last section above doesn't work for titles. Can you revise the program so that it correctly handles a text that includes a capitalized title or even capitalized titles in the body of the text?

4. Notice that split3.pl on page 101 does not handle decimal points properly. Revise it so that it does.

Notes

[1] Octal numbers are base 8. Hence, octal 10 = decimal 8 and decimal 10 = octal 12.

[2] It turns out that all the backslashes aren't really necessary when we construct a regular expression from a string variable. They don't hurt, however, and I include them all for simplicity.

[3] Since $a and $b have this special role for Perl, you should take care *not* to create your *own* variables with the same names!

[4] There are really only two additional symbol types not in the above chart: *, which is used for **typeglobs** (for example, *myglob), and &, which is used for subroutines (for example, &mysub). These are very advanced topics, however, and are not treated in this book.

Chapter 8
HTML

In this chapter, we consider the basics of **HTML**, "HyperText Markup Language". This is the basic formatting language for creating web pages. We treat this here for two reasons. First, one of the strengths of Perl is that it can be used over the web. You can write programs that create web pages dynamically, and that respond to data that is fed to your program from web pages. A second reason is that Perl can be used to retrieve and parse web pages, and this can be a valuable tool for data collection and analysis.

Learning how to create elegant and informative web materials is a huge topic and this chapter will only treat the very basics, only what we need to make efficient use of Perl over the web.

8.1 How the Web Works

The World Wide Web allows computers to exchange a variety of data remotely. The basic model is that of a **server** and a **client**. You and your web browser are the client. Out there, in the electronic ether, are the servers. When you sit at your computer and tell your web browser to connect to some particular **URL**, or web address, you are, in fact, requesting information from a web server. The URL you enter typically includes the name of the server, its location in webspace, perhaps along with an indication of what data you want it to transmit to you. For example, entering a URL such as http://www.bananas.org/plums.html sends a request to the web server located at www.bananas.org to send back the HTML document plums.html.

There are a number of ways the information can be transferred from the server to the client. The one we are concerned with is **HTTP**, or "HyperText Transfer Protocol". This is the format and method by which web-based data is sent back to your web browser. Typically, that information is organized in a specific fashion: **HTML**. In fact, in the above example, the particular bit of data we requested from www.bananas.org was specified as being structured in terms of HTML.

In general, then, the web is a network of web servers, each capable of responding to HTTP requests and sending various kinds of data to web clients. That data is typically structured using HTML.

The other key component to HTML is that the data that is displayed in your browser can contain **links** to other web addresses and data. Selecting one of these links issues a new request to some server for new data, which may, in turn, contain additional links. Hence the term "web".

Those are the central aspects of HTML and the web, but the system is more complex. The example above made it appear as if plums.html was some bit of data already available on the www.bananas.org web server. Such material is referred to as **static content**. This is often, though not always, the case. Sometimes a web server will send data that is constructed specifically in response to the request. This is referred to as **dynamic content**.

It works like this. You, the client, type in a URL at your browser; for example, http://www.bananas.org/plums.cgi. This sends a request to the web server www.bananas.org to send some bit of data. In this case, what actually happens is that a program plums.cgi runs on the web server, constructing some HTML-formatted data, and sends *that* to you, the client. Rather than send you some static saved page, the plums.cgi program constructs some tailor-made data for you. This can be a simple matter of including the current time or date in the returned data, but it can include virtually anything a computer program is capable of producing.

When a web server provides dynamic content, it does so by running some sort of program. There are actually a number of paradigms for doing this, but the most common is called **CGI**, or "Common Gateway Interface". This topic will be treated in depth in chapter 9.

There is a lot more to the web that we can't do justice to in this text. For example, there are other ways of producing dynamic content on a web server; for example, Java servlets, ASP, JSP, and so on. In addition, there are also ways to run programs on the client side; for example, Java applets, JavaScript, Flash, and so on.

8.2   *Basic HTML*

In this section, I introduce the general structure of HTML documents. The basic idea is that a document is a body of text interleaved with **tags**. Tags are HTML code which instructs the web browser how to display the text. In addition, since nontextual material can be inserted in an HTML document, these tags can also instruct the browser where to place images, what kind of background to display, and so on.

HTML tags are quite simple. They are always surrounded by angled braces and usually come in pairs. For example, <html> . . . </html> tells the browser that the text between the tags is encoded using HTML. Note that ending tags are always preceded by a slash; for example, </html>. The <p> tag indicates a paragraph break, and is optionally paired with a </p> tag. The unpaired <hr> tag draws a line across the screen. Here is an example of a typical HTML document:

basic1.html

```
<html>
<head>
<title>A basic page</title>
</head>
<body>
This page has only three things in it. There is a title at the top. There is a
line across the middle of the page below.
<hr>
There is a second paragraph right here.
</body>
</html>
```

This document can be created in your usual text editor. When you open it with your web browser, it displays the following page:

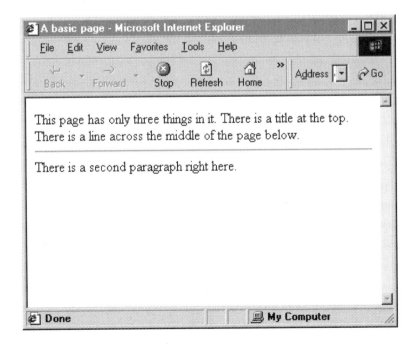

Let's go through the tags that are used in this example. First, there are the surrounding <html> . . . </html> tags, indicating that this is an HTML document. Next, there are the <head> . . . </head> tags. This is where various declarations about the nature of the document go. For our purposes, the only thing that goes here is the title, marked with <title> . . . </title>.

Most of the action in an HTML document will go in the <body> . . . </body> tags. In the example at hand, the <body> tag includes some text and the unpaired <hr> tag. The latter simply separates the text by drawing a line across the screen.

It is important to note that line breaks and the amount of space that separates tags and textual elements are generally irrelevant. Hence, the following HTML code displays exactly like the preceding:

basic2.html

```
<html><head><title>A basic page</title></head><body> This page has only
three things in it. There is a title at the

top. There is a line across the
middle of the page below. <hr> There is a second paragraph
right here.</body></html>
```

The first is better, however, because the line breaks and spacing help reveal the structure of the document.

Let's now go through some of the more useful tags. First, there are the <p> and <br> tags, for breaking text into paragraphs or just to separate lines. The difference is that the former inserts space between the separated text, while the latter does not. Here is an example:

basic3.html

```
<html>
<head>
<title>Line breaks</title>
</head>
<body>
Here is the first line<br>
Here is the second line<br>
A third line<p>
And a fourth line!
</body>
</html>
```

This program produces this output:

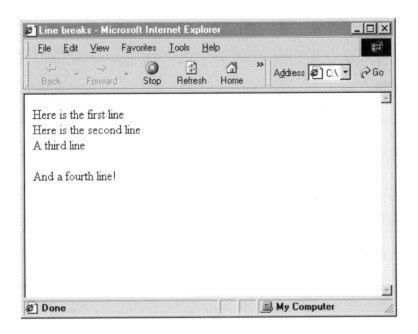

HTML also provides for headings at six different levels. How precisely these are formatted is controlled by settings in the browser. Thus, if you tag some text as being heading level one, <h1> ... </h1>, you can't guarantee precisely how that will display for each user. Typically, it involves a larger typeface and some preceding and following spacing, but this isn't guaranteed. Here is an HTML document that exemplifies all the headings:

basic4.html

```
<html>
<head>
<title>Different headings</title>
</head>
<body>
<h1>heading 1</h1>
Some text.

<h2>heading 2</h2>
More text.

<h3>heading 3</h3>
and more.

<h4>heading 4</h4>
even more.
```

```
<h5>heading 5</h5>
too much.

<h6>heading 6</h6>
way too much.

</body>
</html>
```

Here is how those headings are displayed in my own browser:

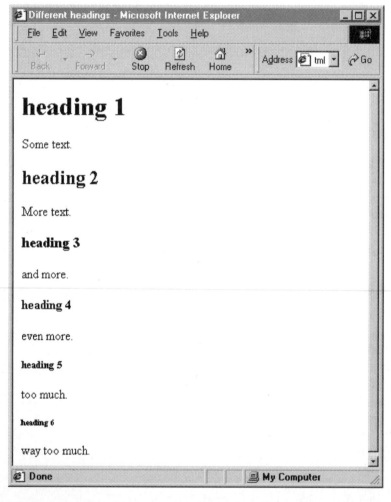

In addition, HTML offers tags for indicating formatting. These can refer either "logical" formatting, like the <strong> . . . </strong> and <em> . . . </em> (for "emphatic") tags, or "specific" formatting, like the <i> . . . </i> (for "italic") and <b> . . . </b> (for "bold"). The logical formatting cannot be guaranteed typographically, but the specific formatting can.

In addition, there is <pre> ... </pre> which turns off all formatting and sets the tagged text in a monospaced font. In this case, line breaks and spaces in the raw HTML *do* matter. Here is an example of all these. The example also includes an instance of the <center> ... </center> tag, for centering text:

basic5.html

```
<html>
<head>
<title>Logical and specific formatting</title>
</head>
<body>
<center>This sentence contains <strong>strong</strong> and
<em>emphatic</em> tags.</center>
<p>
This one has <b>bold</b> and <i>italic</i> text.
<p>
<pre>
Here is some
unformatted    and             very ugly
text.
</pre>
</body>
</html>
```

Here is how this file displays (given the settings for logical formatting in my own browser):

Finally, HTML provides for several different kinds of list structures including ordered lists (tagged with <ol>...</ol>) and unordered lists (tagged with <ul>...</ul>). The latter provide for bulleted lists and the former for numbered/lettered lists. Each allows for embedded lists as well. List items in both cases are marked with the optionally symmetric tag <li>. Here is a simple example of embedded lists of both types:

basic6.html

```
<html>
<head>
<title>Ordered and unordered lists</title>
</head>
<body>
Here are three levels of embedded lists:<p>
<ol>
<li>first item highest level
<li>second item highest level
   <ol>
   <li>first item intermediate level
   <li>second item intermediate level
      <ul>
      <li>first item lowest level
      <li>second item lowest level
      </ul>
   </ol>
</ol>
</body>
</html>
```

Here is how these look:

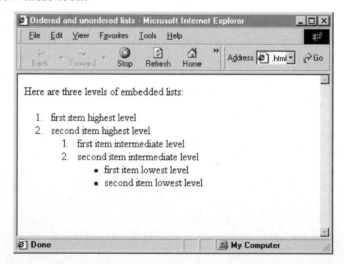

Notice that the tabbing in the source HTML file is totally irrelevant; it is there to help understand the structure of the document and is ignored completely when the HTML is interpreted by the browser.

The list structure given above provides a nice example of an important point about HTML tags. Notice that paired tags can be nested inside each other. Thus, in the previous example, one list is embedded in another embedded in another. It is imperative that such nesting be "proper" when it occurs. Thus the first of the following sequences is an instance of proper nesting and well-formed in HTML. Although it might appear that it should give the same output, the second is not properly nested and will be rejected by your browser:

```
<head><title>A title</title></head>
<head><title>A title</head></title>
```

Finally, certain characters cannot be entered as is, but must be entered using special alternate characters. The most frequently occurring ones are <, >, ", and &. The first two are used to demarcate tags and the last is used itself to signal a special character. To display one of these characters in HTML, you use a special escape sequence. Such sequences always begin with an ampersand and end with a semicolon. Here is a table of the most frequent ones:

```
&lt;      <
&gt;      >
&amp;     &
&quot;    "
```

Here is an example of a file that uses some of these symbols:

basic7.html

```
<html>
<head>
<title>Special characters</title>
</head>
<body>
The &quot;&lt;strong&gt;&quot; tag is used to indicate <strong>important
&amp;
critical</strong> material.
</body>
</html>
```

Here's how this looks:

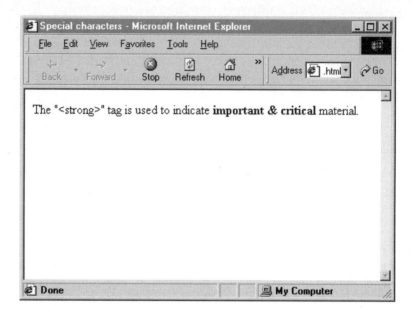

There are many many more tags to HTML and many nuances that are glossed over here, but the above tags are sufficient to exemplify CGI scripts.

8.3   *Mounting Your Pages*

So far, you have created our web pages on your own personal machine and opened them with your own personal browser. To actually put them on a web server, you need to have access to a server. This is typically *not* something you would do with your own personal computer over the phone lines. Rather, to mount your HTML code on the web, you need to get an account on a computer that hosts a web server. If you have an account on a mainframe computer at your work or school, you may already have the power to mount pages on the web. You should contact your computer system administrator to find out if this is so, and how to do this on your own particular system. If you don't have such an account, there are many companies that provide this service. Some even do so for free (in exchange for advertising or similar inducements).

8.4 Links

HTML derives its name from the fact that HyperText can contain **hyper-links**. Hyperlinks are points in an HTML document that can be clicked to take the client to another point in the document, another document or site altogether, or perform some sort of action. In this section, we cover the basics of hyperlinks.

A hyperlink is simply a tag with an added parameter to indicate where the link should take the user. The basic tag is <a> . . . </a>, but it is never used without the added parameter. There are several choices. To indicate where the link should go, the parameter added is href. Its value is indicated by following the parameter with an equals sign followed by its value in parentheses. The text in between the tags indicates what text is highlighted for the user to select to follow the link.

For example, consider the following HTML:

```
<a href="http://www.bananas.org/peaches.html">Peaches</a>
```

This hyperlink displays the text "Peaches". When this link is selected, the browser will make an HTTP connection to the URL indicated. Note that the URL is enclosed in quotes. Here is an example of a page that displays links to all the example pages we have constructed so far:

links1.html

```
<html>
<head>
<title>Sample hyperlinks</title>
</head>
<body>
Here are some sample hyperlinks:<p>
<ul>
<li><a href="basic1.html">Basic tags</a>
<li><a href="basic2.html">Basic tags again</a>
<li><a href="basic3.html">Line breaks</a>
<li><a href="basic4.html">Headings</a>
<li><a href="basic5.html">Formatting</a>
<li><a href="basic6.html">Lists</a>
<li><a href="basic7.html">Special characters</a>
</ul>
</body>
</html>
```

Here is how it looks:

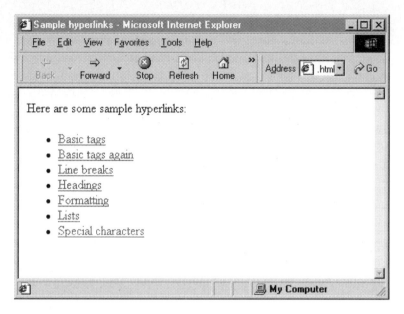

Notice that there is no need to include the name of the web server if the page linked to is on the same server. In addition, the code above assumes that the pages linked to are in the same directory as the links1.html page.

It's also possible to link to a specific location in the same page or a different page. First, the relevant location must be marked with an **anchor** tag. Then the hyperlink must refer to that anchor location. Anchor tags have the following syntax:

```
<a name="anchorname">some text</a>
```

This would create an anchor called anchorname at this location. This could be linked to *within the same document* with the following hyperlink:

```
<a href="#anchorname">some text</a>
```

Clicking on the text in the hyperlink will take the user to the named anchor. If the anchor is in a document called plums.html and the hyperlink is in a different document, then the following hyperlink would work:

```
<a href="plums.html#anchorname">some text</a>
```

Here is a simple example. Here is a simple HTML page with several anchors. The page is a hypothetical discussion of the intricacies of phonology as a discipline:

anchor1.html

```
<html>
<head>
<title>Some anchors</title>
</head>
<body>
<hr>
<h1><a name="phonology">Phonology</a></h1>
```

Phonology is the study of the organization of sounds in a language.
It focuses on the unconscious knowledge a speaker
has of what sounds are possible in their language (<a
href="#inventory">inventory</a>) and how those sounds can be
sequenced (<a href="#phonotactics">phonotactics</a>).

```
<h2><a name="inventory">Inventory</a></h2>
```

For example, English has an aspirated bilabial stop [p], but Spanish
does not. On the other hand, Spanish has a voiced bilabial fricative [β],
but English does not.

```
<h2><a name="phonotactics">Phonotactics</a></h2>
```

For example, words in English can begin with an [s] followed by another
consonant, e.g. [spay] "spy". In Spanish, such words are impossible.

```
<hr>
<h1><a name="phonetics">Phonetics</a></h1>
```

Phonetics is not <a href="#phonology">phonology</a>.

```
<hr>
</body>
</html>
```

The only novel features on this page, other than the anchors, are the follow-
ing. First, this page shows embedded anchors, within formatting commands.
Second, this page provides an example of yet another special character in
HTML: β which is used for β.[1]
   Here is how this page looks:

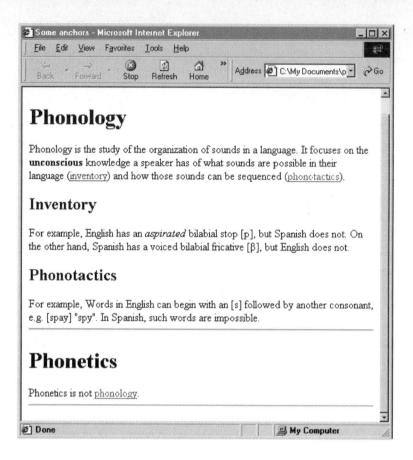

Notice that the anchors are not displayed *per se*. That is, there is no special rendering of text that is marked as an anchor.

Here is a separate page that contains links to the anchors we have placed in the preceding page:

links2.html

```
<html>
<head>
<title>Phonology &amp; Phonetics</title>
</head>
<body>
<h3>Some interesting areas of linguistics</h3>
<ul>
<li><a href="anchor1.html#phonology">Phonology</a>
  <ul>
  <li><a href="anchor1.html#inventory">Inventory</a>
```

```
<li><a href="anchor1.html#phonotactics">Phonotactics</a>
</ul>
<li><a href="anchor1.html#phonetics">Phonetics</a>
</ul>
</body>
</html>
```

Notice how the links to the anchors must refer to the containing page as well, since it is a different page from this one. In addition, no web server address is given, since it is assumed that both pages are in the same directory on the same server.

Here is how this second page looks:

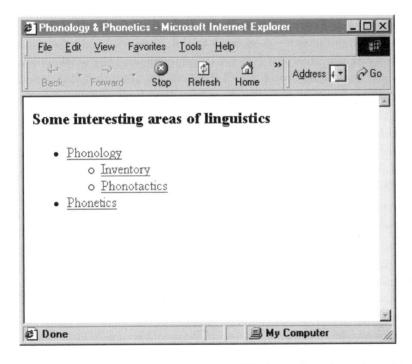

There is much more to say on the topic of links and anchors, but this will suffice to demonstrate the power of Perl CGI scripts.

8.5 *Searching the Web*

In this section, we develop a simple program that searches the web for specific text strings.[2] The basic idea is that the web constitutes a huge repository of language data that we can profitably exploit using Perl. The program described here starts from a single URL, and searches through that page for matches to the search term and any links. If there are matches, they are printed out. The process repeats with any links it finds until it reaches a specified number of matches.

The program makes use of the LWP::Simple module. This is a standard Perl module, but is not necessarily already installed in your Perl system. To check if it is installed in your system, write a program that includes a use statement with this module name. If that runs satisfactorily, then the module is already installed. If not, then you may be able to install it yourself from the source files at www.cpan.org.[3]

The program below does a certain amount of work parsing HTML code; that is, separating HTML tags from text. There are actually free Perl modules that do this as well, but for our purposes here, there would actually be more overhead to learning how to use these modules than writing the parsing code ourselves.

Let's consider the general logic of the program. It is invoked with three command-line arguments: a URL, a search term, and the maximum number of hits. The main data structures of the program are two arrays: one to keep tabs on links found that haven't yet been checked, and the other to keep track of links that have already been checked (so they aren't checked twice).

Starting with the seed URL given on the command line, the program goes through the HTML page extracting matches with the search term and adding links to the set of links to be checked. The only real complexity comes from checking that any new links added haven't already been checked.

Let's now go through the program step by step. The program begins with a use statement, signalling to Perl that it can make use of the LWP::Simple module. This module has a single function that we want: get(), which will retrieve a web page given a URL argument. Next we initialize several variables: $linkmax for the maximum number of pending links, @urlstodo to hold the links to check, $pattern to hold the search term, and $hitmax to hold the maximum number of hits:

websearch.pl

```perl
use LWP::Simple;

if ($#ARGV != 2) {
    die("usage: perl websearch.pl URL pattern hits\n");
}

$linkMax = 50;
push(@urlstodo, $ARGV[0]);
$pattern = $ARGV[1];
$hitmax = $ARGV[2];
. . .
```

The body of the program is a while-structure that iterates over the links in the @urlstodo array checking for the search term and adding new links when they are found. The loop ends when there are no more links to check or the appropriate number of hits have occurred.

Each time through the loop, a counter holding the number of links checked is incremented. There is then an if-structure that prints an update message to STDERR every ten links. The current URL is put in a local variable $theURL and added to the list of URLs already done. The contents of the URL are retrieved with the get() function of the LWP::Simple module. The text returned by get() is then split into separate lines which we iterate through. If the pattern is matched, the URL and line are printed. If the line contains a link to an HTML document, we use a defined subroutine addURL() to add it to @urlstodo:

```
. . .
while ($hits < $hitmax and $#urlstodo > -1) {
    $linksChecked++;
    if ($linksChecked % 10 == 0) {
        print(STDERR "Checked: $linksChecked\n");
    }
    $theURL = pop(@urlstodo);
    push(@done, $theURL);
    $mycontent = get($theURL);
    if ($mycontent) {
        @lines = split(/\n/, $mycontent);
        foreach $line (@lines) {
            if ($line =~ /$pattern/) {
                print("$theURL:\t$line\n\n");
                $hits++;
            }
            if ($line =~ s/^.*(href|HREF)="([^"]+html?)".*$/\2/) {
                addURL($theURL, $line);
            }
        }
    }
}
. . .
```

The addURL() subroutine takes two arguments: the current URL and the new link. It does three things. First, it checks if the link is relative to the current URL. If it is, it reconstructs the full URL using the current URL as a base. Next, it checks if the link is already in @urlstodo or @done. If it is, then the subroutine exits without doing anything further. If it isn't in either of those arrays, it is added to @urlstodo:

```
. . .
#adds the url to the list of urls if it's not already there and hasn't already
#been checked.
sub addURL {
  my($url);
  if ($#urlstodo < $linkMax) {
    my($prefix) = shift();
    my($suffix) = shift();
    if ($suffix !~ /^http/) {
      if ($prefix =~ /\/$/) {
        $suffix = $prefix . $suffix;
      } else {
        $suffix = $prefix . "/" . $suffix;
      }
    }
    foreach $url (@done) {
      if ($suffix eq $url) {
        return();
      }
    }
    foreach $url (@urlstodo) {
      if ($suffix eq $url) {
        return();
      }
    }
    push(@urlstodo, $suffix);
  }
}
```

Notice finally, that there is a maximum to @urlstodo. This keeps the program efficient, as the number of links can grow very quickly.

8.6   *Summary*

This chapter has introduced the basics of HTML, "HyperText Markup Language". We discussed the workings of the web and presented much of the structure of HTML. We presented the basic tags for structuring and formatting a web page and introduced the tags for hyperlinks and anchors. We have also developed a program that runs over the web for retrieving, parsing, and searching web pages. In the next chapter, we will make use of all of this to develop Perl programs that run over the web in the other direction.

8.7 *Exercises*

1. Create a web page that defines and exemplifies all the tags we have used.
2. Write a program that will convert logical to specific formatting *and vice versa.*
3. Write a program that will concordance an HTML document.
4. Write a program that will strip all HTML tags from a document.
5. Write a program that will check an HTML page for proper nesting.
6. Write documentation for the preceding program in HTML.

Notes

[1] This is the symbol in the International Phonetic Alphabet for a voiced bilabial fricative.

[2] This program is inspired by work of Will Lewis: "The web as linguistic resource: methods for harvesting and analyzing linguistically relevant data off the web", manuscript, University of Arizona.

[3] See appendix D. The module is already preinstalled in the ActiveState™ Perl distribution for Windows. If you're working on a large multi-user system, you should ask the system administrator to install it for you.

Chapter 9

CGI

In this chapter, we treat **CGI**, or "Common Gateway Interface" programming. We can write Perl programs that run over the web in response to user queries.

This is a complex topic, but the advantages are so dramatic that it is definitely worth covering. Running a program over the web allows you to collect or display data remotely. It allows you to make use of HTML for graphical interfaces and allows you to draw on – or present your data to – a virtually limitless mass of people.

The basic idea is that when a web client makes a request of a web server, that server runs a Perl program, rather than sending back some specific fixed bit of information.

9.1 CGI Access

So far, we have been writing programs that you can run on your own personal computer, or on a mainframe computer on which you have an account. CGI scripting requires that you have access to a web server.

It's important to note that putting CGI scripts on the web is not as simple as putting HTML on the web. CGI scripts are quite powerful and present serious security concerns for a computer system administrator. If you have a web site, you should check with your system administrator to see if you are allowed to put CGI scripts on the web.

If you do, there are two principal ways to do this. One possibility is that you are required to place your CGI scripts in a special directory, typically cgi-bin. Another possibility is that while you can put your CGIs in the same place as your HTML files, you must suffix your CGIs with a special suffix, typically .cgi. In either case, there are three central steps to putting CGI scripts on the web. First, you must determine if you have permission to do so. Second, you must determine the particular configuration of your web server and how it manages CGI scripts. Third, you must write your script so that the web server invokes it with Perl, rather than some other programming language. All three issues should be resolved with your computer system administrator.[1]

In this chapter, I will assume that you have what appears to be the most frequent setup. CGI scripts can be stored under any name, but must be stored in a special directory cgi-bin. To force them to be invoked with Perl, the first line of the program must be #!/usr/local/perl, where this expression includes the path of your Perl interpreter.[2]

9.2   *Simple CGI*

Here is a maximally simple CGI program. All it does is print out a simple page announcing its existence:

`cgi1.pl`

```
#!perl

print("Content-type: text/html\n\n");

print("<html><head><title>First CGI!</title></head><body> \n");
print("You've reached my <strong>first</strong> ");
print("CGI program.</body></html>");
```

On my own system, this program would be invoked with this URL:

http://hammond.ling.arizona.edu/cgi-bin/cgi1.pl

There are several important things to notice about this program. First, as indicated in the preceding section, it begins with the statement #!perl, which is necessary for some web servers. Second, the first thing the program does is print out a statement that is not displayed by the browser. This statement is something that is sent covertly by the web server when it displays an HTML page. If your CGI program is displaying HTML content, then it must send this line first *exactly as is*, including the two final returns. Here is how this document looks:

HTML involves lots of extra formatting and using Perl print() statements to print it all out can result in ungainly line lengths or many prints. A convenient alternative is to use **here-document** syntax.[3] Any number of lines can be grouped into a string with the << operator. First, you define a string-terminating string. In the example below, I use HTML. Then you decide whether you want to double-quote or single-quote the whole expression. If you want to double-quote the whole expression, then the multi-line string begins with <<"HTML", and the final line must be HTML. If you want to single-quote the whole expression, then the multi-line string beings instead with <<'HTML'. Note that there should be no space between << and HTML, and the final HTML must appear on a line all by itself. (Single- and double-quoting here works the same way as with other strings.)

The following program uses here-document syntax to produce the same output as the preceding program:

`cgi2.pl`

```perl
#!perl

print(<<'HTML');
Content-type: text/html

<html>
<head>
```

```
<title>First CGI!</title>
</head>
<body>
You've reached my <strong>first</strong> CGI program.
</body>
</html>
HTML
```

The here-document syntax can be used in all other sorts of Perl programming as well.

So far, CGI programs are not any more useful than HTML. The following HTML page will of course display the same thing as the preceding two CGI programs:

fakecgi.html

```
<html>
<head>
<title>First CGI!</title>
</head>
<body>
You've reached my <strong>first</strong> CGI program.
</body>
</html>
```

Where CGI programs have a real use is when *dynamic* content is called for. A very simple example of this is a program that displays the current time.

To do this, we make use of the localtime() command. The command is actually quite powerful and has several options. If it is given no argument, it automatically takes the output of time() as its argument. (Recall that time() returns the number of seconds since January 1, 1970.) If it occurs in a context where it should only return a single value, then it returns a string displaying the current date and time. If, on the other hand, it occurs in a list context, then it returns a nine-member list holding all the specifics of the current time. The following table shows these nine values:

0	seconds
1	minutes
2	hours (24-hour clock)
3	day of the month
4	month (0–11)
5	year (four digits)
6	day of the week (0–6)
7	day of the year (1–366)
8	daylight savings (0 or 1)

This is a very useful set of information, but for our purposes, it suffices to simply return the simple string.

The following CGI program displays the local time and date in response to an HTTP query:

cgi3.pl

```perl
#!perl

$date = localtime();

print(<<"HERE");
Content-type: text/html

<html>
<head>
<title>What time is it?</title>
</head>
<body>
The time here is: $date.
</body>
</html>
HERE
```

The program begins by assigning the current time to a variable $date. Then it uses here-document syntax to construct the HTML and print it. Since we want to interpolate the variable, we put double quotes around the first HERE. Here's how the CGI displays:

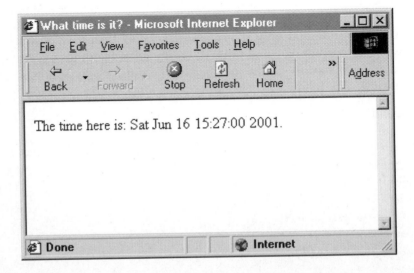

Try this yourself. Make sure to hit your browser's reload button several times and note how the time is updated each time the program is run. This is, of course, what we would expect of a program running on the server. Moreover, this kind of behavior is impossible in a static HTML document.

9.3   Finding CGI Errors

Working with CGI programs can be quite difficult, because when there is an error in your program the web server does not display the error at the command line. Typically, if your CGI program has some sort of error, the web server will add that error to its general "error log". Finding the error log and finding your own program's error in that log can be quite difficult.

It is therefore useful, during development, to have errors displayed in your web browser. This can be done by adding the following line near the beginning of your CGI program:

```
use CGI::Carp('fatalsToBrowser');
```

This command instructs Perl to display any CGI errors in the web browser by making use of the CGI::Carp module (standardly included in all Perl implementations). If you use this, don't forget to remove this line once your program is running properly.

9.4   HTTP Requests

Any information available to a program running on the server is available to your CGI program. However, it also can obtain information about the client, the machine making the request. All of this information is automatically available to your program through the %ENV hash. In fact, this hash structure is available to normally running programs as well. Here is a program that will display the elements of %ENV along with their values for a normal program:

`env1.pl`

```
foreach $key (keys(%ENV)) {
   print("$key\t$ENV{$key}\n");
}
```

These values include all the environment variables set for you in your operating system. They typically include the type of prompt, your working path, and other similar information.

The following CGI program displays %ENV on a web page:

env2.pl

```perl
#!perl

print("Content-type: text/html\n\n");

print("<html><head><title>ENV information</title><head><body><ol>\n");

foreach $key (keys(%ENV)) {
   print("<li>$key\t$ENV{$key}\n");
}

print("</ol></body></html> \n");
```

The keys that show up when %ENV is accessed by a CGI program are somewhat different, including various information about the HTTP connection. For our purposes, the most important keys are these: PATH_INFO, QUERY_STRING, and REQUEST_METHOD. Let's go through these.

The REQUEST_METHOD key should have the value GET. This is the kind of HTTP request being responded to. All normal HTTP requests are GET requests. We will see below that there are also POST requests, and that these are also quite useful.

The PATH_INFO key may not actually show up when you invoke env2.pl as you would expect. If, however, you suffix the CGI name in the URL with any further hypothetical path information – for example, /linguists – then that information will show up as the value for PATH_INFO. For example:

http://hammond.ling.arizona.edu/cgi-bin/env2.pl/linguists

Try this with env2.pl with different choices (substituting the correct server name for your CGI programs). Notice that this additional path structure must *follow* env2.pl in the URL. If it precedes it, then the server will not be able to find your CGI program.

Finally, the QUERY_STRING key displays any information that follows the CGI name separated by a question mark. For example:

http://hammond.ling.arizona.edu/cgi-bin/env2.pl?linguists

Again, try this yourself with different values after the question mark. As with PATH_INFO, this information must follow the CGI program name. Otherwise, the server will not be able to find the CGI program.

The difference between PATH_INFO and QUERY_STRING is immaterial at this stage, but is significant when we treat forms below.

9.5 Using Links to Interact

Let's now show how you can use PATH_INFO[4] to handle more substantive information transfer over the web. Here's a rather silly example of how we can use PATH_INFO to run our Pig Latin program (page 89) as a CGI program. Here is the code:

piglatincgi.pl

```perl
#!perl

print(<<'HEAD');
Content-type: text/html

<html>
<head>
<title>Pig Latin CGI</title>
</head>
<body>
HEAD

if (exists($ENV{PATH_INFO})) {
   $word = $ENV{PATH_INFO};
   $word =~ s/^\///;
   print("You entered <strong>$word</strong>.<p> \n");
   print("The Pig Latin form is: ");
   $c = "[bcdfghjklmnpqrstvwxzBCDFGHJKLMNPQRSTVWXZ]";
   $v = "[aeiouyAEIOUY]";
   if ($word =~ /^[yY]?($v.*)$/) {
      print("$1-yay");
   }elsif ($word =~ /^($c+)(.*)$/) {
      print("$2-$1ay");
   }
   print(".<p>\n");
}else {
   print("You didn't enter a word in the URL!<p> \n");
}

print(<<'TAIL');
</body>
```

```
</html>
TAIL
```

As usual, the program begins with #!perl. It then uses here-document syntax to print out the HTML header. It then checks if %ENV has a PATH_INFO key. If it does, then it assigns the value to a variable $word. The leading slash is stripped off and the program prints out the word entered. The central logic of the program is lifted straight from piglatin1.pl. If there is no PATH_INFO key, if no word was entered after the program name in the URL, the program informs the user of that. Finally, the remaining HTML is printed.

Here is an example of how the program is invoked (on my own server):

http://hammond.ling.arizona.edu/cgi-bin/piglatincgi.pl/saguaro

And here is the output:

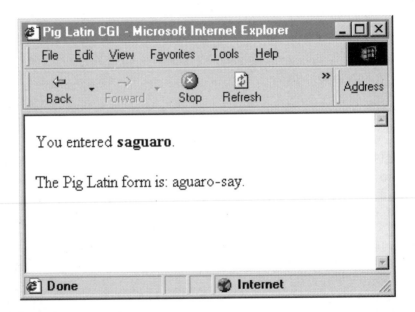

This program is somewhat awkward, since the word to be converted has to be entered as part of the URL. Let's give another program where the information in the URL is provided in another way. The following program is a first attempt at running experiments over the web.

For demonstration purposes, the experiment is a very simple one. The user is presented a series of words and asked to judge the number of syllables in each word. The user will be presented with a web page, with appropriate instructions and a series of links to indicate their choice. Here's an example of what this display looks like:

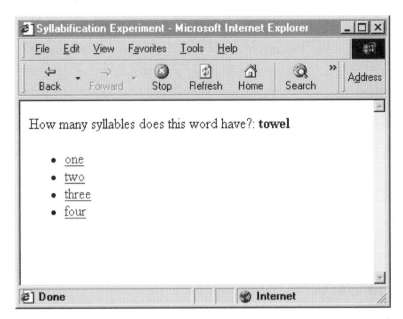

Each response is a hyperlink where the particular response triggers the next item and records the user's response to the current item.

The key to making this system work is to keep in mind that the web server and CGI program may be interacting with many users at the same time. Thus, we must have a system in place that keeps track of what items a user has already seen and what their responses to those items were.

The program below does this by updating the PATH_INFO value every time a response is made. When a user makes their response and selects a hyperlink, that hyperlink will include in the PATH_INFO part of the URL what the current response is and what the preceding responses have been. In this way, the CGI program will be able to send back an item that that user hasn't seen yet, or end the experiment when the user has responded to all items.

What we need then is a way of encoding what items a user has seen and what their responses have been. To do this, the following program encodes each item as a two-digit number and each response as a single-digit number. The PATH_INFO part of the URL is then a series of numbers; for example, /032051003, where every three digits encodes an item–response pair. In the current example, we can break the string up as follows: (03-2)(05-1)(00-3). This subject has seen items 3, 5, and 0, and has given the responses 2, 1, and 3, respectively.

Let's now look at the code. There are a number of interesting bits, so we'll go through this one slowly. The program begins with the usual #!perl declaration required for CGI programs. It then sets several variables. The @words array is for the experimental items. Each time we check the PATH_INFO key for which items the current user has already seen, we will do so by stripping out items from the @words array. Later, we will still need access to the original order of items, so we make an immediate copy in @wordssave. The third variable is just to keep track of the address of the current CGI:

expcgi1.pl

```perl
#!perl

@words = ("hat", "towel", "cowl", "flour", "flower", "happy", "charity");
@wordssave = @words;
$mycgiurl = "http://www.bananas.org/cgi-bin/expcgi1.pl";
. . .
```

Next comes a rather large nested if-structure. At the outermost level, it tests if the current request has a value specified for the PATH_INFO key. If it does, then the experiment has already begun. If it has not, then there is an else-clause to begin the experiment.

If the PATH_INFO key exists, then the subject has already completed some items. In that case, we need to determine which items they have completed and if there are any remaining items. If there are remaining items, then a new item must be selected and presented. The first few lines then use pattern-matching to figure out which items have already been presented. They do this by creating a new array of indices from the item numbers recovered from the PATH_INFO string. It then pops off items that have already occurred from the original @words array. If any items remain, then the next item is chosen from this set. If no items remain, then a final message is displayed and the data is stored in a file on the server:

```perl
. . .
if (exists($ENV{PATH_INFO})) {
    #get results up to this point
    $res = $ENV{PATH_INFO};
    $res =~ s/^\///;
    $ressave = $res;
    while (length($res) > 0) {
        $res =~ s/^(\d\d)\d//;
        $already = $1;
        push(@nums, $already);
    }
    @nums = sort(@nums);
    while ($#nums > -1) {
        $already = pop(@nums);
        splice(@words, $already, 1);
```

```
}
#are there still items to run?
if ($#words > -1) {
   $thisword = getrandom();
   displayItem($thisword);
#if there are no more items; end of experiment
} else {
   #save results to file
   open(F, ">>cgi-res.txt") or die("Can't open results file!\n");
   my($date) = localtime();
   print(F "$ressave\t$date\n");
   close(F);
   thankyou();
}
} else {
   #begin experiment
   $thisword = getrandom();
   displayItem($thisword);
}
. . .
```

Notice how file IO is as you would expect. You should be careful here, though. There are occasionally different limits put on what and where a CGI script can write to. You should make sure that your CGI program uses explicit path information for each file it needs, and you should test your CGI program to make sure it can actually read and write where you want it to.[5]

There are three subroutines invoked by the program. The getrandom() subroutine selects a random item from the (remaining) items in @words:

```
. . .
sub getrandom {
   my($ind) = rand($#words + 1);
   return($words[$ind]);
}
. . .
```

The displayItem() subroutine first recovers the original index of the current item from the @wordssave array. It then corrects this index if necessary, so that all item numbers in PATH_INFO are two digits long. Finally, it prints out the HTML code. This code includes hyperlinks that are tailor-made to where this particular subject is in the experiment. Each hyperlink includes the items and responses up to now and then adds on the current item number and the appropriate response code:

```
. . .
sub displayItem {
    my($item) = shift();
    for ($k = 0; $k <= $#wordssave; $k++) {
        last if ($wordssave[$k] eq $item);
    }
    $k = '0' . $k if (length($k) == 1);
    print(<<"HTMLEND");
Content-type: text/html

<html>
<head>
<title>Syllabification Experiment</title>
</head>
<body>
How many syllables does this word have?: <strong>$item</strong><br>
<ul>
    <li><a href="$mycgiurl/$ressave${k}1">one</a>
    <li><a href="$mycgiurl/$ressave${k}2">two</a>
    <li><a href="$mycgiurl/$ressave${k}3">three</a>
    <li><a href="$mycgiurl/$ressave${k}4">four</a>
</ul>
</body>
</html>
HTMLEND
}
```

Notice the curly braces in the hyperlinks surrounding the $k variable. This is so that Perl doesn't try to interpret that variable as $k1, and so on. Notice too that variables are possible in the here-document print statement because the initializing terminator HTMLEND is given in double-quotes.

Finally, there is a subroutine thankyou() that prints out an appropriate message at the end of the experiment:

```
. . .
sub thankyou {
    print(<<"THANK");
Content-type: text/html

<html>
<head>
<title>Syllabification Experiment</title>
</head>
<body>
```

```
<strong>Thank you!</strong>
</body>
</html>
THANK
}
```

This is a reasonable approach to providing specific information to a CGI without having to enter it in the URL overtly. Here, the hyperlinks add this information to the URL covertly.

However, this approach doesn't generalize to all cases. We also want to be able to handle cases where the set of possible user responses is unbounded, where the user can enter anything in response to a CGI query.

9.6   *HTML Forms*

A form is an HTML structure that includes various sorts of **GUI** ("graphical user interface") objects such as buttons, checkboxes, and textfields.[6] A user can respond to these objects and this information is then sent back to the web server for some program there to respond to. In this section, we explain how to construct these forms.

A form is an arrangement of GUI elements along with other HTML code, grouped together with at least one GUI object to submit the data collected by the form. The form tag itself <form> . . . </form> surrounds the form. The leading tag requires two attributes be specified in the tag. The first required attribute is action which specifies what CGI program is to run on the data submitted; this information is given as a URL. The other required attribute is method which must be set to either GET or POST. The method attribute specifies how the data is transmitted to the program. Data submitted via GET are put in the QUERY_STRING key of %ENV. Data submitted via POST are read from STDIN. We will give examples of both of these techniques.

Here is an example of the form tag:

```
<form action="http://www.bananas.org/myprog.cgi" method=GET>
. . .
</form>
```

The action attribute here indicates that when the enclosed form data is submitted, it is submitted to a program called myprog.cgi which is located on the www.bananas.org web server. The method attribute indicates that the data will be submitted via the GET method.

Let's consider the very simplest kind of form. There is a single GUI object for entering a string of text, and a button to submit the data to the CGI program. Here is the HTML:

form1.html

```
<html>
<head>
<title>Simple form</title>
</head>
<body>
<form action="http://www.mysite.org/myprog.cgi" method=GET>
Enter your name in the box:<p>
<input type="text" size=30 name="mytext1">
<hr>
<input type="submit" value="Tell us your name">
</form>
</body>
</html>
```

There are the usual tags for <html>, <head>, <title>, and <body>. Then there are the form tags indicating what the program is and where it is, and also that the GET method is used. Here's what the form looks like:

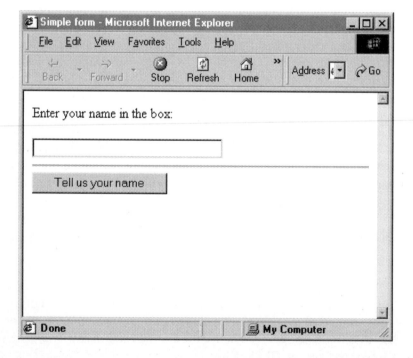

Within the form, there are two GUI objects: a text box and a submit button. The former is simply a box in which the user can insert some text. It takes two attributes here. The size attribute says how many characters wide the box is. The name attribute gives the name of the variable that the contents of the text box are associated with.

It is quite easy to write a CGI program that responds to the form1.html form. The following program simply displays the value of QUERY_STRING taken from %ENV in response to form1.html:

f1cgi.pl

```perl
#!perl

print(<<"THEHTML");
Content-type: text/html

<html>
<head>
<title>Responding to a form</title>
</head>
<body>
<strong>Here is the query string</strong>:<br>
$ENV{QUERY_STRING}
</body>
</html>
THEHTML
```

If I enter my own name in the form1.html text field (remembering to first change the action parameter so that it references this CGI program), f1cgi.pl displays the following window:

The information entered in the text field is returned in the QUERY_STRING key. The variable name we assigned to the text field in form1.html precedes the equals sign and the information entered follows it. Note how the space between my first name and my last name is encoded in the QUERY_STRING as +. All sorts of special characters, spaces, and whatnot have to be encoded specially by a form so that they can be sent as part of the URL. While a space is encoded as +, most other special characters are encoded as a unique hexa-decimal (base 16) number preceded by %.[7] For example, & is encoded as %26. Any special processing you have to do of the information entered in the form should take account of this encoding.

Some webservers put a limit on the amount of information that can be included as part of a URL, typically something on the order of 256 charac-ters. If your form is to return that much information or more, you should use the POST method instead. Here is a slight revision of form1.html that makes use of the POST method:

form2.html

```
<html>
<head>
<title>Simple form using POST</title>
</head>
<body>
<form action="http://www.mysite.org/myprog.cgi" method=POST>
Enter your name in the box:<p>
<input type="text" size=30 name="mytext1">
<hr>
<input type="submit" value="Tell us your name">
</form>
</body>
</html>
```

The only change here is that the method parameter is specified instead as POST.

Responding to the POST method involves slightly more work. As I indi-cated above, input from a form with the POST method comes to the CGI program via STDIN, so you might quite reasonably expect to be able to collect that input with <STDIN>. This will not work though. The problem is that the input from the POST method is not terminated by a return, so <STDIN> won't get it. To read this input in, we must use the read() function. This function reads in a specified amount of information from some file handle. In the case at hand, the CONTENT_LENGTH key of the %ENV hash holds the length of the input. The read() function takes three arguments: the file handle, a variable to put the input, and the number of characters to read. The following CGI program exemplifies:

f2cgi.pl

```perl
#!perl

read(STDIN, $stuff, $ENV{CONTENT_LENGTH});

print(<<"THEHTML");
Content-type: text/html

<html>
<head>
<title>Responding to the POST method</title>
</head>
<body>
<strong>Here is the input </strong>:<br>
$stuff
</body>
</html>
THEHTML
```

The output of this program is (essentially) identical to that of the preceding one. The only substantive difference is that this latter program makes use of POST, and far more information can be sent via a form.

So far, we have only included a single text field, and so very little information has been sent. However, there are a number of other GUI objects available in a form and we now go through some of these.[8]

Forms allow for checkboxes and radiobuttons. These are useful when the user is to respond "yes" or "no" to some set of items. Use checkboxes if the choices are not mutually incompatible and radioboxes if the choices are mutually incompatible. Here is a form that presents a set of three checkboxes:

form3.html

```html
<html>
<head>
<title>Checkboxes</title>
</head>
```

```
<body>
<form action="http://www.mysite.org/myprog.cgi" method=GET>
What languages do you speak?<br>
<ul>
<li>Basque<input type="checkbox" name="Basque">
<li>Navajo<input type="checkbox" name="Navajo">
<li>Something else<input type="checkbox" name="Else">
</ul>
<input type="submit">
</form>
</body>
</html>
```

Here is what the form looks like when several of the checkboxes have been checked:

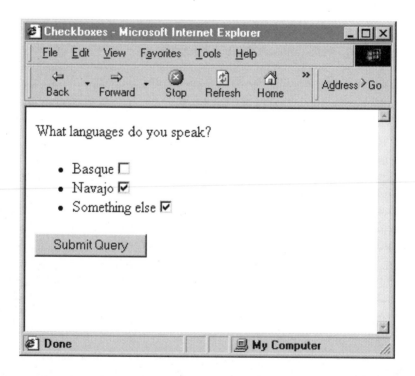

If we pass the form request to f1cgi.pl above, it displays the following information:

Notice how checked checkboxes are included in the query string as checkbox-name=on. Notice too how if there are multiple GUI objects in a form, the different values are separated by &.

Radiobuttons are quite similar and are used when the choices are mutually exclusive. Here is a form that exemplifies this:

form4.html

```
<html>
<head>
<title>Radiobuttons</title>
</head>
<body>
<form action="http://www.mysite.org/myprog.cgi" method=GET>
What language do you speak best?<br>
<ul>
<li>Basque<input type="radio" name="lang" value="Basque">
<li>Navajo<input type="radio" name="lang" value="Navajo">
```

```
<li>Something else<input type="radio" name="lang" value="Else">
</ul>
<input type="submit">
</form>
</body>
</html>
```

Notice that the input type here is radio. Notice also that the name and value attributes are used differently here. The name attribute defines what variable will hold the resulting choice. Since these three radioboxes form a mutually exclusive set, they all share the same name. The value attribute holds the value that is reported if that checkbox is selected. Here is what the form looks like if "Navajo" has been selected:

If, once again, we feed this through f1cgi.pl, we get this display:

Another extremely useful GUI object is a text area, which allows the user to enter a larger block of text. Text areas get their own symmetric tags, including several attributes. The rows and cols attributes allow one to specify the number of rows and columns (in characters), and the name attribute supplies a variable name for the input returned. In addition, any text between the tags is placed as default text in the text area. Here is a simple example:

form5.html

```
<html>
<head>
<title>A text area</title>
</head>
<body>
<form action="http://www.mysite.org/myprog.cgi" method=GET>
Describe the language situation in your home.<p>
<textarea rows=5 cols=30 name="sit">
Put your description here!
</textarea>
<hr>
<input type="submit">
</form>
```

```
</body>
</html>
```

This displays as follows:

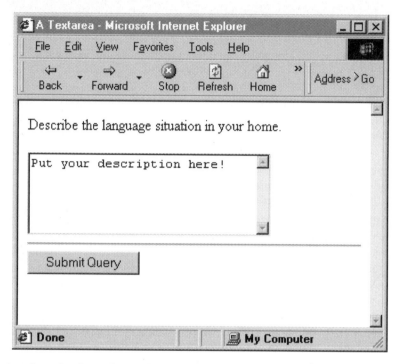

Here is what the form looks like when we've entered some (unfortunately!) fictitious language information:

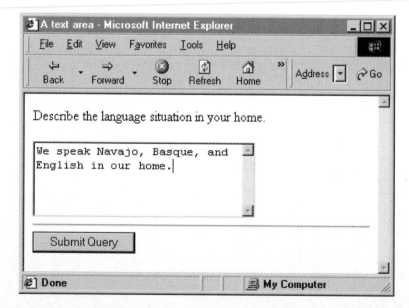

If this is fed through f1cgi.pl, we get the following results:

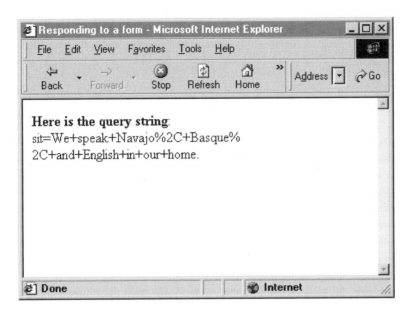

Note how most of the punctuation is encoded using special character sequences (as described above).

Other GUI objects and many other attributes are available, but the ones above should suffice to exemplify how Perl can be used with forms to collect language data over the web. Here is a table summarizing all the GUI objects and attributes we have gone over:

	Objects	Attributes
Submit	input type="submit"	Submit input
	value	Text on button
Text	input type="text"	Single line of text
	size	Width in characters
	name	Variable name
Checkbox	input type="checkbox"	Mutually compatible
	name	Variable name
Radiobutton	input type="radio"	Mutually incompatible
	name	Variable name and radio set
	value	Value returned for name
Text area	Symmetric tags	Multiple lines of text
	rows	Height
	cols	Width in characters
	name	Variable name

9.7   *Running an Experiment Over the Web*

To see forms in action, let's now revise the expcgi1.pl program using forms. We actually need three programs here. The first is a CGI program to randomize items and display a form interface for the subject to enter his or her response in. The second is another CGI program, this time to save the results to a file. Finally, we give a third program for parsing the results file.

Here is the first program, the one for randomizing and displaying a form interface for indicating a subject's syllabification choices. The program has four main bits, separated into distinct subroutines:

expcgi2.pl

```perl
#!perl

@words = ("hat", "towel", "cowl", "flour", "flower", "happy", "charity");

randomizeWords();
doHeader();
doItems();
doEnd();
. . .
```

Experimental items are randomized, and then a form is constructed to collect the user's responses. Here is the randomizeWords() subroutine:

```perl
. . .
sub randomizeWords {
    my($word, @temp, $ind);
    while ($#words > -1) {
        $ind = rand($#words + 1);
        $word = splice(@words, $ind, 1);
        push(@temp, $word);
    }
    @words = @temp;
}
. . .
```

That method makes use of familiar bits.

Next is the doHeader() subroutine. This method prints out the beginning of the HTML page and the beginning of the form. Notice how we use a POST method here:

```
. . .
sub doHeader {
   print(<<'HEADER');
Content-type: text/html

<html>
<head>
<title>Syllabification experiment</title>
</head>
<body>
<h4>For each of the items below, indicate the number of syllables:</h4>
<form action="http://www.mysite.org/cgi-bin/saverescgi.pl" method=POST>
<ol>
HEADER
}
. . .
```

The doItems() subroutine creates a set of radiobuttons for each randomized item:

```
. . .
sub doItems {
   foreach $item (@words) {
      print(<<"ITEM");
<li><strong>$item</strong><br>
1<input type="radio" name=$item value=1>
2<input type="radio" name=$item value=2>
3<input type="radio" name=$item value=3>
4<input type="radio" name=$item value=4>
ITEM
   }
}
. . .
```

Finally, the doEnd() subroutine prints out the end of the form and the HTML:

```
. . .
sub doEnd {
   print(<<'MYEND');
</ol>
<input type="submit" value="submit responses">
</form>
```

```
</body>
</html>
MYEND
}
```

Here's what all this looks like:

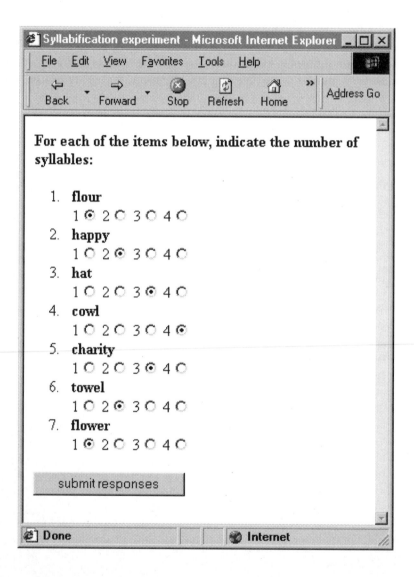

Note that the order of items is random, and each invocation of the CGI program results in a different ordering.

The expcgi2.pl program creates a form that sends its input to yet another CGI program savecresgi.pl. This program saves the results to a file expres.txt, and displays an appropriate message in the subject's browser:

saverescgi.pl

```perl
#!perl

read(STDIN, $results, $ENV{CONTENT_LENGTH});

$date = localtime();

open(F, '>>expres.txt') or die("oops!\n");
print(F "$date\t$results\n");
close(F);

print(<<'MYHTML');
Content-type: text/html

<html>
<head>
<title>Thank you!</title>
</head>
<body>
Thank you for participating in our experiment!
</body>
</html>
MYHTML
```

The results are saved each to a separate line with the time and date indicated first on each line. Here is what the file looks like after four (fictional) subjects:

```
Sun Jul 1 12:03:35 2001 flour=1&happy=2&hat=3&cowl=4&charity=3&towel=2&flower=1
Sun Jul 1 12:34:41 2001 hat=1&cowl=1&flour=1&charity=3&flower=2&towel=2&happy=2
Sun Jul 1 12:34:57 2001 charity=3&happy=3&towel=2&flour=1&hat=1&flower=1&cowl=1
Sun Jul 1 12:36:16 2001 flour=1&cowl=1&charity=3&happy=2&towel=1&flower=2&hat=1
```

As usual, the results are encoded. If we want to make use of them, we need to write some code to parse the different values from the string. I give such a program now. In the real world, we would want to massage our results into a form suitable for statistical analysis. However, in this case, for simplicity, the program simply calculates the average for each item.

parsecgires.pl

```perl
open(F, 'expres.txt') or die("oops!\n");

$subject = 0;

while ($line = <F>) {
   chomp($line);
   ($date, $string) = split(/\t/, $line);
   @items = split(/&/, $string);
   $subject++;
   foreach $item (@items) {
      ($word, $syllables) = split(/=/, $item);
      $results{$word} += $syllables;
   }
}

close(F);

foreach $key (sort(keys(%results))) {
   $avg = $results{$key} / $subject;
   print("$key\t$avg\n");
}
```

The code here is rather straightforward, but demonstrates the kind of parsing necessary to make sense of input to a CGI program. We use the split() function on & to find items, and then again on = to separate variables from values.

For a more detailed statistical analysis, we would want to massage our results into a form that can be submitted to some statistical analysis program. Delimiting data points with tabs is a very common form accepted by many software packages; for example, Excel, SPSS, and so on. The following program exemplifies:

parsecgires2.pl

```perl
open(F, 'expres.txt') or die("oops!\n");

$subject = 0;

while ($line = <F>) {
   chomp($line);
   ($date, $string) = split(/\t/, $line);
```

```
@items = split(/&/, $string);
$subject++;
foreach $item (@items) {
    ($word, $syllables) = split(/=/, $item);
    $results{$word}= $syllables;
}
print($subject);
foreach $key (sort(keys(%results))) {
    print("\t$results{$key}");
}
print("\n");
}

close(F);
```

Notice how by using sort(), each column represents a distinct item.

9.8   *A Glitch*

There is actually a technical problem with some of the CGI programs we have written so far. The problem specifically has to do with those CGI programs that write to some file. The problem arises because, when responding to requests, a web server generates any number of "copies" of a single CGI running in memory at the same time. The problem occurs when several different programs, or instances of the same program, attempt to write to the same file at the same time.[9] Unpredictable data loss can obtain if this occurs.

It is possible in Perl to "lock" a file in use so that other programs, or program instances, must wait until the file is unlocked. The relevant command is flock() and it takes a filehandle and an integer constant as arguments; for example, flock(F, LOCK_EX). When you close the file later in the program, the lock is released and the file becomes available to other programs.

There are two further complications, however. First, the flock() command provided by Perl is not guaranteed to do this. The flock() command in the Fcntl package, however, *is* guaranteed to do this. Therefore you must specify at the beginning of your program that you will be invoking the flock() command of the Fcntl package; for example, use Fcntl ':flock';.

The second complication is that since flock() takes a filehandle as an argument, the file must be opened before it can be locked. It is possible for conflicts to occur in that interval. To avoid this, you should use a dummy **semaphor** file to lock out other programs or program instances. The following revision of saverescgi.pl exemplifies:

saverescgi2.pl

```perl
#!perl

use Fcntl ':flock';

read(STDIN, $results, $ENV{CONTENT_LENGTH});

$date = localtime();

open(MYLOCK, '>mylock.sem') or die("Can't make lock\n");
flock(MYLOCK,LOCK_EX);
open(F, '>>expres.txt') or die("oops!\n");
print(F "$date\t$results\n");
close(F);

close(MYLOCK);

print(<<'MYHTML');
Content-type: text/html

<html>
<head>
<title>Thank you!</title>
</head>
<body>
Thank you for participating in our experiment!
</body>
</html>
MYHTML
```

This is just like the original program except for the addition of four lines. First, we add the use statement so that we invoke the correct version of flock(). Second, we open a new filehandle MYLOCK linked to a dummy semaphor file mysem.sem. Running the program will actually create this file, but it will have no contents. We then lock the semaphor's filehandle before manipulating the file we are actually inteested in: expres.txt. After we close that file, we then close MYLOCK, releasing the lock.

9.9   Summary

This chapter has introduced the topic of CGI programming. Exactly how you write and deploy a CGI program depends a great deal on the kind of web server and computer architecture you are using. We introduced the basic logic and essential bits of CGI programming under any assumptions.

We went over how to use a CGI program to generate dynamic web content, and we introduced here-document syntax to print out multi-line HTML.

We then went on to cover forms. We introduced a number of GUI objects for collecting input from a user, and we showed how that input could be treated either via the POST or GET methods. In addition, we showed how to generate forms themselves dynamically with our final expcgi2.pl program.

Before concluding this chapter, we should touch briefly on security. CGI programs are potentially quite dangerous. They run by remote control in response to user input that you may not anticipate. This means that you should exercise caution in what your CGI programs do, and that you should spend some time thinking about the most wild sorts of information your user might enter into the forms you write. The kinds of programs we've been developing here are all perfectly safe, but there are some very unsafe things that you can do as well. It is an unfortunate fact that there are people out there who try to break into computer systems. Be careful that your CGI programs are not their entry into your system.

Here is a very obvious case of an egregious security lapse. Imagine you have a CGI program that responds to a form interface taking text entered into a text area and assigning it to a variable $mystring. The program then executes the command system($mystring). The problem is that your CGI program thus allows *any* web surfer the rights to execute *any* command on your system: a *very* bad idea.

9.10 *Exercises*

1. Write a CGI program that makes use of all the GUI objects we have discussed.
2. Write a CGI program that takes HTML code as input (in a text area) and strips out the HTML.
3. The expcgi2.pl program presents stimuli all in one pass. Rewrite the program so that it presents experimental items one by one, in random order, using a form interface.
4. Write a new kind of experiment that will run as a CGI program, using a form interface.

Notes

[1] It is not possible to try out CGI programming without a web server. However, it is possible to run a web server on your own personal computer. This won't put your

HTML or CGI programs on the web, but it will allow you to test out and play with CGI programming.

2 On my own computer, my own path is available to the web server, so this expression can be kept maximally simple: #!perl.

3 This mysterious term comes from Unix shell script usage.

4 Or 'equivalently' QUERY_STRING.

5 For example, under Unix, you may need to run the chmod command with the flags a+rw so that you have complete access to your file.

6 These are treated in a non-CGI context in appendix B.

7 Hexadecimal numbers use the following digits: 0, 1, 2, 3, 4, 5, 6, 7, 8, 9, A, B, C, D, E, F.

8 All of these can be used with either GET or POST methods.

9 This problem and the solution that I discuss below were drawn to my attention by Sean Burke. For more discussion, see Sean Burke, "Resource locking with semaphor files", *SysAdmin/The Perl Journal*, 2002.

Appendix A
Objects

This appendix treats the topic of **objects** and **object-oriented programming** (OOP) in Perl. This is a huge and complex topic, and we can only scratch the surface here. OOP is not really essential to make use of most of the power of Perl. Thus, none of the preceding chapters have required objects. We have therefore relegated this topic to an appendix.

There are several important reasons to treat the topic, though. First, OOP offers several conceptual attractions as compared to traditional "procedural" programming of the sort we have covered up to now.

In addition, there are a number of extremely useful publicly available Perl modules that require familiarity with OOP to make use of them. For example, appendix B introduces the **Tk** module which allows for graphical user interfaces in Perl. It is impossible to build graphical user interfaces in Perl without a basic understanding of OOP.

A.1   Object-Oriented Programming

To understand object-oriented programming, it helps to compare it with orthodox procedural programming. Procedural programming means organizing your programs in terms of tasks, in terms of a series of function calls and subroutine invocations.

OOP involves a radically different approach. The basic idea is that programs are organized in terms of "things". There are still function calls and subroutine invocations, but they are now simply the "glue" that ties the objects together.

Let's consider an example. Let's take the case of a program that reads textual data from a file, tokenizes it into words, builds a concordance, and prints the concordance to the screen. There are a number of ways to implement this procedurally. Here's one:

procex1.pl

```
open(F, $ARGV[0]) or die("Oops!\n");

while ($line = <F>) {
   @words = split(/\b/, $line);
   while ($#words > -1) {
      $word = pop(@words);
      $conc{$word}++;
   }
}

close(F);

foreach $key (sort(keys(%conc))) {
   print("$key\t$conc{$key}\n");
}
```

There are, of course, lots of other ways this can be done, but this will suffice for present purposes.

Let's now consider how this might be recast in OOP terms. Here, we lay out how to do this in general, leaving the details for later in the appendix. Again, there are a number of ways to do this. We'll choose a relatively simple one to just illustrate the general OOP idea.

First, we would define an object File. The File object will handle opening a file and provide methods for reading data. These tasks would be accomplished *inside* the File object, and would not be visible to other objects in our program. We'll also define an object Line which we build from the File object. We can do this using the **methods**, or subroutines, of these two objects. The call to split() would be put in a method of the Line object. Finally, the Concordance object would hold the final concordance of the document. It would provide methods or subroutines for constructing the concordance and for returning or printing out its contents.

The key idea here is **data encapsulation**. Each object we have proposed is responsible for manipulating its own particular set of data. For example, the File object would handle the string which gives the name of the file to be read from and the filehandle that the file is associated with. Likewise, the Line object would handle the strings associated with each line from the file. Presumably, it would also provide for splitting each line into individual words.

What data encapsulation does is provide a programming model that forces the programmer to separate conceptual components of the program appropriately. It allows one to "hide" data. Thus the data manipulated internally by each object are hidden from other objects, the data are encapsulated.

This discussion has been rather abstract, and the purported advantage of OOP somewhat mysterious. Once we have explained the machinery of Perl objects, we can really understand their virtues.

Let's understand the machinery of Perl objects a little more concretely. You, as programmer, will write separate blocks of code for each of the objects you define. Each object will include data structures and subroutines of two types: **public** and **private**. Public data structures and subroutines are created for the object to interact with other objects. Private data structures and subroutines are meant for the private and "hidden" use of the object.

In addition, your object should provide a **constructor** subroutine, the steps taken when your object is first created.

A.2   References

To understand objects and constructors, we must first understand **references**. We go over references briefly in this section.

References are a different kind of variable. They provide a mechanism for referring *indirectly* to the contents of a variable.

Let's look at a simple example. Let's take a variable $myVar and assign it the value "hat". We can convert this variable to a reference with the **indirection** operator \; that is, \$myVar. If we assign \$myVar to another variable – say, $myRef – then $myRef is now a reference. We can retrieve the value of the reference by prefixing it with a *second* $: $$myRef. Here is a small program showing how this works:

`ref1.pl`

```
$myVar = $ARGV[0];
$myRef = \$myVar;
print("$$myRef\n");
```

The value of $myVar is taken from the command line. Using the backslash, $myRef becomes a reference to that variable. Using a second $, the value of the reference is printed, the value originally entered on the command line.

This "dereferencing" with $ is general. We can also create references to hashes and arrays, and they are dereferenced with @ and % as we would expect. Here is a small program that shows how this works with an array:

`ref2.pl`

```
$arr[0] = $ARGV[0];
$arr[1] = $ARGV[1];
```

```
$myRef = \@arr;
print("$$myRef[0]\n");
print("$$myRef[1]\n");

@arr2 = @$myRef;
print("$arr2[0]\n");
print("$arr2[1]\n");
```

First, the contents of @arr are initialized from the command line. A reference to this array $myRef is created by backslashing @arr. The individual array elements are retrieved with $. Next, the *entire* array is dereferenced with @, and assigned to @arr2. Individual elements of that array can be accessed normally. The program shows how a reference to an array can be created, and how dereferencing can take place at different levels.

Here's a program showing the same thing for hashes:

ref3.pl

```
$myHash{$ARGV[0]} = 1;
$myHash{$ARGV[1]} = 2;

$myRef = \%myHash;
print("$ARGV[0]\t$$myRef{$ARGV[0]}\n");
print("$ARGV[1]\t$$myRef{$ARGV[1]}\n");

%hash2 = %$myRef;
print("$ARGV[0]\t$hash2{$ARGV[0]}\n");
print("$ARGV[1]\t$hash2{$ARGV[1]}\n");
```

First, the keys for a hash %myHash are taken from the command line and assigned simple values. A reference to that hash is created with backslash. Then the individual hash key–value pairs are retrieved using $. The entire hash can also be dereferenced with %, and then its key–value pairs are accessed normally.

Using array and hash references actually comes up quite often, so there is another way to get access to the array or hash elements of a reference: ->. This operator is placed in between the reference name and the array index or hash key to return the value of that element. Here is an example:

arrow1.pl

```
@myArray = ('Catalan', 'German', 'Quechua', 'English');
$myRef = \@myArray;
```

```
for ($i = 0; $i <= $#{$myRef}; $i++) {
   print("$i\t$myRef->[$i]\n");
}

$myHash{Catalan} = 'Spain';
$myHash{German} = 'Germany';
$myHash{Quechua} = 'Peru';
$myHash{English} = 'USA';
$myOtherRef = \%myHash;
foreach $key (sort(keys(%$myOtherRef))) {
   print("$key\t$myOtherRef->{$key}\n");
}
```

This program creates an array and a hash of language names (and countries). It then assigns a reference to both. The array reference is stepped through using the -> operator, rather than using @ or $. Likewise, the hash reference is also stepped through using the -> operator. We will use this operator extensively when we turn to objects in the next section.

So far, references seem to have little utility. However, for complex programming, they are extremely useful. The key aspect to a reference is that it stores a variable, not a value. Hence, if a reference is created to some variable, and the value of that variable changes, then the value of the reference also changes. Here is a deliberately tricky program showing how this works:

ref4.pl

```
$hat = $ARGV[0];

print("\$hat = $hat\n");

$chair = \$hat;
$couch = $hat;

print("\$\$chair = $$chair\n");
print("\$couch = $couch\n");

$hat = $ARGV[1];

print("The new value of \$hat = $hat\n");
print("\$\$chair = $$chair\n");
print("\$couch = $couch\n");
```

This is an especially confusing program to make sense of. The thing to keep in mind is that backslash has *two* uses here. When used in a string, backslash escapes following special character. Thus, in a string, \\$ simply prints $. Outside of a string, backslash is used for indirection, as in the previous examples in this section.

This program shows how a reference holds onto the variable it has been assigned to even when the value of that variable changes. In this program, we take two values from the command line and assign them both to $hat. Let's imagine that the first command-line argument is "apple". The program first assigns that value to $hat and then prints it out. It then creates a reference to $hat: $chair. It also assigns the value of $hat directly to $couch. Both of these are then printed out, and each of course has the value "apple".

Next, the value of $hat is changed to the second command-line argument, say "orange", and printed out. The reference to $hat is printed out next and it too has the value "orange", since it is a reference to $hat. On the other hand, when $couch is printed out, it retains the original value of "apple", since it was simply assigned the value of $hat, and was not a reference to $hat.

This, of course, can be very confusing, but it can also be quite useful for advanced programming tasks.

Another central aspect of references is that they allow hashes and arrays to be treated as simple variables. This is quite useful as well. For example, using references, you can put hashes into arrays or arrays into hashes. Imagine, for example, that you want to create a data structure to store what country different languages are spoken in, and you want to allow for the case that some language is spoken in more than one country. You have the following sort of information:

Language	Countries
French	France, Canada, and so on
English	USA, Canada, England, and so on
Tohono O'odham	USA, Mexico
Spanish	Spain, USA, Mexico, and so on

For language names, you really want a hash, but for each list of countries, you want an array. This can be done readily with references. The basic idea is that each list of countries will be put into an array. We then create a hash with language names as keys and *references* to arrays (of country names) as values:

ref5.pl

```
@frCountries = ('France', 'Canada');
$myData{French} = \@frCountries;
@enCountries = ('USA', 'Canada', 'England');
$myData{English} = \@enCountries;
```

```
@toCountries = ('USA', 'Mexico');
$myData{'Tohono O\'odham'} = \@toCountries;

foreach $key (sort(keys(%myData))) {
    print("$key:\t@{$myData{$key}}\n");
}
```

This program simply initializes the data structure and then prints out its contents. Notice first how quotes are required around Tohono O'odham because the language name includes a quote character which must be escaped.[1] Second, note how curly braces are required when dereferencing the array here so that the scope of the dereferencing is clear.

Notice how each array must be given its own name. This is fine for a simple case like this where the language names are known in advance, but would break down in a larger program where the language names are not given in advance. This situation is common enough that Perl provides a mechanism for creating an anonymous array reference [] or an anonymous hash reference {}. Here is the same program revised to use anonymous array references:

ref6.pl

```
$myData{French} = ['France', 'Canada'];
$myData{English} = ['USA', 'Canada', 'England'];
$myData{'Tohono O\'odham'} = ['USA', 'Mexico'];

foreach $key (sort(keys(%myData))) {
    print("$key:\t@{$myData{$key}}\n");
}
```

Here, the square brackets convert a list of items into an anonymous array reference.

In fact, we can also initialize the hash with a list, which simplifies the assignment even more. In the following, we use the => operator. This does exactly the same thing as a comma, but shows the paired structure of the hash more clearly:

ref7.pl

```
%myData = (French => ['France', 'Canada'],
    English => ['USA', 'Canada', 'England'],
    'Tohono O\'odham' => ['USA', 'Mexico']);

foreach $key (sort(keys(%myData))) {
    print("$key:\t@{$myData{$key}}\n");
}
```

Here the hash is initialized with a list, where each pair of items in the list is taken as a key–value pair. Those pairs are (unnecessarily) separated with =>, rather than comma. The value for each pair is an anonymous array reference in square brackets.

We have seen that references provide another way to store values. Using references allows us to refer to specific variables, rather than simply to the content of those variables. We've seen that references allow us to create some powerful new data structures.

References are quite powerful and we can do lots more with them. They are, however, a complex topic and we have only introduced them so that we can make sense of objects. We therefore leave the topic here, and turn to objects directly.

A.3   Basic Syntax

Once we have references, objects in Perl are actually quite simple to construct. An object is simply a set of subroutines and data structures grouped together into a package which includes a subroutine whereby variables can be blessed into objects. Perl includes a special function bless() that returns a reference to a specific object.

Let us try to understand this with a very simple example:

`obj1.pl`

```perl
package MyObj;

sub new {
    my($self) = {};
    my($class) = shift();
    bless($self, $class);
    return($self);
}

sub doSomething {
    print("Success!\n");
}
```

This program defines an object type – or **class** – called MyObj. The class includes two subroutines. The first is a constructor for the class and is called when an instance of the class is first created. The second is simply a test subroutine – or **method** – of the class.

Let's go through the new method. All object definitions should include such a method, and the parts here are fairly standard. First, the new() method defines a reference of some type, here a reference to a hash. Second, the class name (also the package name) is obtained from the anonymous array that subroutine arguments come from. Third, the bless() function is used to turn the hash reference into an object of the type MyObj. Finally, that object is returned.

The second subroutine simply prints out a message.

In and of itself, this class definition doesn't do anything. An object must be defined as being of the MyObj type, and then it can do something. Here is a minimally revised version of the preceding program that actually does something:

obj2.pl

```perl
$hat = MyObj->new();
$hat->doSomething();

package MyObj;

sub new {
    my($self) = {};
    my($class) = shift();
    bless($self, $class);
    return($self);
}

sub doSomething {
    print("Success!\n");
}
```

The class definition is the same, but here it is preceded by code that instantiates the class and then invokes its substantive method. First, the $hat variable is instantiated as a reference to an object of type MyObj by invoking its new() method. Notice how -> is used to retrieve the new() method of the MyObj class. That method returns a reference which is then assigned to $hat. The doSomething() method is also accessed through the -> operator, and it prints out the message.

So far, objects don't really do anything special. We could have done just the same thing if the first two lines of the program above were simply replaced with MyObj::doSomething(). However, objects are things that have an existence over the duration of your program. The following program exemplifies this:

`obj3.pl`

```perl
$hat = MyObj->new();
$time = time();
do {
   $timediff = time() - $time;
} while ($timediff < 3);
$hat->doSomething();

package MyObj;

sub new {
   my($date) = localtime();
   my($self) = {myData => $date};
   my($class) = shift();
   bless($self, $class);
   return($self);
}

sub doSomething {
   my($self) = shift();
   my($date) = localtime();
   print("This object was created:\t$self->{myData}\n");
   print("The time now is:\t$date\n");
}
```

This program differs from the preceding one in several ways. First, it initializes $hat, and then uses a while-structure to wait for three seconds. Then it invokes the doSomething() method of the $hat object.

The new() method now includes some extra code so that the anonymous hash reference now contains a key myData which contains the date and time the method was run.

The doSomething() method now collects a reference to the current object from the anonymous array. (The current object is always the first element of that array.) It then collects the current time. It uses the reference to the current object to retrieve the time the object was created and compares that with the current time just retrieved.

This program shows several things. First, it shows that the anonymous hash blessed into the object can actually contain useful key–value pairs that can be accessed by subroutines/methods of the class. Second, it shows how the object has some autonomous "existence". It can contain its own data and manipulate that data.

A.4 Using Objects

Let's now use objects to revise the concordance program (see page 174). We have already gone through the logic of this program above. The basic idea is to make a simple concordance of a file. First, we create a File object to store the file being concordanced. Next, we use that object to initialize a Concordance object. The Concordance object opens the file, and creates Line objects of each line. It then uses the methods of the Line class and its own to construct a concordance, which it prints out.

Let's now go through the details:

concObj.pl

```
$file = File->new($ARGV[0]);
$myConc = Concordance->new($file);
$myConc->printIt();
. . .
```

The program begins by creating a new File object, and assigning it to $file. Next, the File object is used to create a Concordance object. Finally, the concordance is printed using its own printIt() method. Note that both the File and Concordance constructors take arguments, given in parentheses after new.

Let's now go through the different class definitions required to make this work. First, there is the File class, a minimalist class designed to show the basic architecture. It has two subroutines. The new() method first takes two arguments from @_: the name of the class, and the $filename argument. It then defines $self as an anonymous hash reference with one key–value pair. That one pair designates the filename. Next, it blesses $self into the File class, and returns a reference.

The File class includes a second method that simply returns the name of the file. It does this by first obtaining a reference to the current class, and then using that reference to access the anonymous hash that the object is built on. This may seem fairly silly. After all, the filename information is available directly from the anonymous hash reference. However, to enforce data encapsulation, one doesn't usually allow external access to that hash structure. Instead, one should write explicit **accessor** methods like this one to make internal data available in a controlled fashion:

```
. . .
package File;

sub new {
    my($class) = shift();
```

```
    my($filename) = shift();
    my($self) = {filename => $filename};
    bless($self, $class);
    return($self);
}

sub getFile {
    my($self) = shift();
    return($self->{filename});
}
. . .
```

The next class is the Line class, which provides methods for breaking up a line of text into word tokens. The constructor for this class takes a string of text as an argument, and provides a method to tokenize that string. The constructor first finds two arguments in @_: its class name and the text string it's given as an argument. The final return of that text string is stripped off by chomp(), and then $self is defined as a hash reference containing a single key text with the text string as its value. The method then blesses $self as a Line, and then returns the reference.

The other method of the Line class is getTokens(), which returns an array of words from the text string. The method first determines the invoking object from @_, and then uses that reference to find the text string that the object was created with. It then uses split() to tokenize the string and returns the tokens as an array:

```
. . .
package Line;

sub new {
    my($class) = shift();
    my($text) = shift();
    chomp($text);
    my($self) = {text => $text};
    bless($self, $class);
    return($self);
}

sub getTokens {
    my($self) = shift();
    my($text) = $self->{text};
    my(@words) = split(/\b/, $text);
```

```
    return(@words);
}
```
. . .

The final and most important class of the program is the Concordance class, which holds the concordance and has methods for creating and accessing it.

The first method is new() which first finds its class, and then finds its single File argument. It then blesses $self into a Concordance object and calls its makeIt() method. That method takes a single string argument designating the file. That string is supplied by the getFile() accessor method of the File class. Finally, the constructor returns the reference to the created object:

. . .
```
package Concordance;

sub new {
    my($class) = shift();
    my($file) = shift();
    my($self) = {};
    bless($self, $class);
    $self->makeIt($file->getFile);
    return($self);
}
```
. . .

The makeIt() method takes two arguments from @_: a reference to the invoking object, and the string argument. It then opens the file and reads through it line by line. Each line is used as a string argument to a new Line object. Then those Line objects are taken as arguments to the Concordance class's addWords() method:

. . .
```
sub makeIt {
    my($self) = shift();
    my($file) = shift();
    open(F, $file) or die("Can't open file");
    while (<F>) {
        my($line) = Line->new($_);
        $self->addWords($line);
    }
    close(F);
}
```
. . .

The addWords() method takes two arguments: the object reference and the reference to the Line object. It uses the getTokens() method of the Line object to retrieve the words of the line, and then it adds those words to the hash representing the concordance, adding new keys or augmenting existing values as appropriate:

```
. . .
sub addWords {
   my($self) = shift();
   my($line) = shift();
   my(@words) = $line->getTokens();
   foreach $word (@words) {
      $self->{$word}++;
   }
}
. . .
```

Finally, the printIt() method of the Concordance class allows the concordance to be printed out:

```
. . .
sub printIt {
   my($self) = shift();
   foreach $key (sort(keys(%$self))) {
      print("$key\t$self->{$key}\n");
   }
}
```

This program may seem fairly complex. Recasting it in OOP style has resulted in a much larger program with a lot more code than the original procedural program (page 174). On the other hand, the object-oriented version of the program has a very clear structure.[2]

A.5   *Summary*

This appendix has introduced the complex notion of object-oriented programming (OOP). Objects are not strictly necessary to accomplish most anything you'd want to accomplish with Perl, but we introduce this topic for two reasons. First, there are some conceptual advantages to OOP. If you are already familiar with another object-oriented language, for example Java™, you may prefer OOP. Second, there are some very standard Perl modules that use OOP. You need to understand OOP to make use of those modules.

For example, as noted at the beginning of this chapter, you cannot create graphical user interfaces in Perl without OOP.

We began with an introduction to the notion of references, variables that refer not directly to values, but to the variables that contain those values. We then went on to show how the bless() function, in conjunction with the package declaration, allows for OOP in Perl.

Use objects with care. While they are conceptually appealing, they entail a lot more coding in most cases. In addition, in Perl, there are huge time efficiency losses when programming with objects; whatever the virtues of OOP, object-oriented Perl programs run more slowly.

Notes

[1] A glottal stop. In point of fact, in the official orthography of the language, the word is 'O'odham, "people", with two glottal stops.
[2] One of the main virtues of OOP is **inheritance**. We do not treat this very advanced topic here.

Appendix B

Tk

Perl was not originally designed as a "graphical language", but most modern computer programs now include some sort of graphical user interface, or GUI. The Tk module was developed as a mechanism for providing GUIs for Perl. We have already seen that HTML can be used as a GUI for Perl, when run over the web. There is another way, as well, to provide a GUI for your Perl programs: the Perl **Tk** module. The Tk module is a set of objects and methods that provide windows, buttons, text entry fields, and so on for a Perl program. It is extremely powerful and, in its most basic form, rather easy to use.[1]

To make use of Tk, you really need to know how to use objects in Perl. So if you skipped over appendix A, you need to go back and read it now!

B.1 Installing Tk

The Tk module does not come automatically with every Perl installation. It needs to be installed separately. If you are using ActiveState™ Perl on a Windows machine, it is extremely easy to install. In other cases, it can be a major undertaking.

First, you should check if it is already installed on you machine. You should use the use statement to invoke the Tk module. If Perl does not complain, the module is already installed. If Perl complains that it cannot find Tk in @INC, then you need to install it. The simplest way to check is to enter the following at your command line perl -e "use Tk" (for Windows) or perl -e 'use Tk' (for Unix). The -e flag causes Perl to run the following command-line argument as a one-line program.

Windows. If you are using ActiveState Perl on a Windows machine with fast internet access, installing Tk is quite easy. This version of Perl provides a

command-line program for adding optional modules to your Perl installation. Simply type ppm at the command line. This starts the "perl package
manager" program. When you get the ppm prompt, type install Tk. This will
then connect your machine to the internet to install the Tk module. This is a
very big download and will take some time over a slow connection. When
the installation is complete, simply type exit.

Unix/Linux. To install Tk on a Unix-type machine is a hugely complex
enterprise. If you are working on a multi-user machine with a professional
system administrator, ask that person to install it for you. If you are on a
single-user machine, it can be as simple as finding a pre-built binary for your
specific architecture, or it can involve compiling a very large number of files
from scratch. Finally, note that to make use of Tk under Unix, you need
access to X-windows, or a similar windowing environment.

Macintosh. The Tk module is not currently available for MacPerl. There
are some similar MacPerl windowing functions, but nowhere near what Tk
provides. Up to MacOS 9, Tk is not available yet.[2]

The Tk module usually comes with an impressive demo program called
widget, which exemplifies virtually all of the Tk GUI elements. To see it, type
widget at your command line after Tk is installed.

B.2   Building a GUI

There are several steps to creating a GUI using the Tk module. First, you
must define a set of GUI objects: buttons, windows, text fields, and so on.
Second, you must lay those objects out in your program window using Tk's
geometry management functions. Third, you must assign functions to the
relevant user interface devices. That is, you must write the code for what
happens when you click your button, and so on.

Let's look at a very simple example to see how this is done:

gui1.pl

```
use Tk;

$mywin = MainWindow- > new();
$mybutton = $mywin- > Button(-text => "Done", -command => sub { exit() });
$mybutton-> pack();

MainLoop();
```

First, there is a use statement warning Perl that you will be using the Tk module. Next, there is a line declaring that $mywin is an object of the MainWindow type. As you were warned above, the Tk module makes liberal use of Perl OOP. The MainWindow class provides routines for constructing other GUI objects of various types. The next statement in the program defines $mybutton as an object of the Button type, associated with $mywin. The constructor takes a list of arguments, which are passed in "hash-style". These arguments are used to set basic properties of the Button object. The first pair sets the text that appears on the button. The second pair sets the subroutine that is executed when the button is pressed. The next statement places the button in the window. Finally, the MainLoop() statement instructs the program to wait for a GUI event and respond accordingly. In this case, the program will simply display a small window with a button, which will close when the button is pressed. Here is what the program looks like:

The basic idea, then, is that we use object style to create a set of GUI objects. These are then positioned in a window. In the next sections, I will go over how to position these objects, some of the objects available, and how to write subroutines that respond to these objects. In the final section of this appendix, I give a graphical version of the syllable-counting experiment using Tk GUI elements.

B.3   Geometry Management

Tk GUI elements, or **widgets**, can be placed in a window by a variety of "geometry management" functions. These enable one to place widgets in incredibly precise and intricate ways. Unfortunately, geometry management with Tk is a complex topic and so in this section I outline only the simplest GUI placement function: pack().

We have already seen the pack() function in action in the gui1.pl program above. What it does is place a widget along the top edge of the enclosing window, sizing the window so that the natural size of the widget can be displayed. Multiple widgets are placed successively below preceding ones in the order their pack() statements are executed. The following program shows three buttons all placed with pack():

gui2.pl

```
use Tk;

$mw = MainWindow->new();
$mw->Button(
    -text => 'Button 1',
    -command => sub { exit() })->pack();
$mw->Button(
    -text => 'Button 2',
    -command => sub { exit() })->pack();
$mw->Button(
    -text => 'Button 3',
    -command => sub { exit() })->pack();

MainLoop();
```

As with the preceding program, this one begins with a use statement warning Perl that we will be using the Tk module. Then we create a new MainWindow and assign a reference to it to $mw. We then invoke the Button method of MainWindow to create a Button widget associated with $mw. This button displays the text string specified and is packed in the default manner. Two more buttons are added in the same way and then the MainLoop() eventloop command is given, causing Perl to wait for a GUI event.

Notice here that the buttons are created and packed with a single statement each, unlike the previous program where the button is created, a reference is assigned, and then the reference is used to pack the button.

Here's what the display looks like:

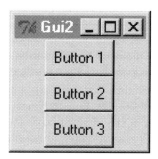

We can actually add arguments to pack() that specify what side a widget is packed up against: left, right, top, or bottom. Here is a program showing four buttons packed up against the four different sides:

`gui3.pl`

```perl
use Tk;

$mw = MainWindow->new();
$mw->Button(
    -text => 'top',
    -command => sub { exit() })->pack(-side => 'top');
$mw->Button(
    -text => 'bottom',
    -command => sub { exit() })->pack(-side => 'bottom');
$mw->Button(
    -text => 'left',
    -command => sub { exit() })->pack(-side => 'left');
$mw->Button(
    -text => 'right',
    -command => sub { exit() })->pack(-side => 'right');

MainLoop();
```

The only difference here is that pack() takes a pair of arguments, the first of which specifies that the -side parameter is being set, and the second of which is its value. Here's what the display looks like:

Here, the order in which elements are packed makes a difference. For example, if elements are packed clockwise from the top, we get this display:

Here's the code:

`gui4.pl`

```
use Tk;

$mw = MainWindow->new();
$mw->Button(
  -text => 'top',
  -command => sub { exit() })->pack(-side => 'top');
$mw->Button(
  -text => 'left',
  -command => sub { exit() })->pack(-side => 'left');
$mw->Button(
  -text => 'bottom',
  -command => sub { exit() })->pack(-side => 'bottom');
$mw->Button(
  -text => 'right',
  -command => sub { exit() })->pack(-side => 'right');

MainLoop();
```

You might try different orders with these to see the different effects. You can also pack multiple items up against the same side and achieve yet other effects. I leave working through all these to the exceptionally careful reader.

As I mentioned at the outset, there are many many more intricate details to how widgets can be arranged in a window. We have only scratched the surface here.

B.4   Widgets

The Tk module offers a number of GUI objects, and this section discusses several of these: Button, Label, and Radiobutton.

B.4.1   Button

We've already seen several invocations of the Button widget. The -text parameter sets the text string that is displayed, and the -command parameter sets the subroutine that is run when the button is pressed. There are several other useful parameters as well.

An extremely useful parameter is the -textvariable parameter, which design-ates a reference to a variable that holds the text displayed by the button. Whenever that variable is changed, the text displayed by the corresponding button is changed. Here is a program that shows how this works. This pro-gram displays two buttons, the first of which toggles through two different text strings:

`gui5.pl`

```perl
use Tk;

$b1text = "yes";

$mainw = MainWindow->new();
$b1 = $mainw->Button(
    -textvariable => \$b1text,
    -command => sub {
        if ($b1text eq "yes") {
            $b1text = "no";
        } else {
            $b1text = "yes";
        }
    });
$b1->pack();
$mainw->Button(-text => 'quit', -command => sub { exit() })->pack();

MainLoop();
```

Here, we invoke Tk as usual, and set the value of a variable $b1text to "yes". We then create a MainWindow as usual. We define a button $b1 setting the -textvariable parameter to the *reference* \$b1text. We set the -command vari-able to be a somewhat longer anonymous subroutine. This one checks if $b1text equals "yes", and sets its value accordingly. We add a second button to quit the program.

Here's what it looks like:

It's also possible to set the color of Buttons, the MainWindow, and virtually every other widget. Most GUI elements have a parameter -background for their basic background color. Buttons also have an -activebackground parameter. A Button will change color when the mouse passes over it, and this parameter controls that color.

A huge number of colors are available; if you want to see a full list, invoke the widget Tk demo (by typing widget at the command line), where there is a list of available colors on your system. Here's a small revision of the gui1.pl program where we've set the various color possibilities using the two parameters above:

gui6.pl

```
use Tk;

$mywin = MainWindow->new(-background => 'blue');
$mybutton = $mywin->Button(
   -text => 'Done',
   -command => sub { exit() },
   -background => 'red',
   -activebackground => 'green');
$mybutton->pack();

MainLoop();
```

Notice that the -background parameter is set both by the MainWindow constructor new() and by the Button() method. Since the images in this text are given in grayscale, the display of this program would look just like that of gui1.pl.

B.4.2   Label

Another very useful widget is the Label, which can be used to display text. Its text can be set with -text or with -textvariable. Here is a simple example:

gui7.pl

```
use Tk;

$countmsg = $count++ . " presses";

$mwin = MainWindow->new();
$mwin->Label(-text => "Press the button")->pack();
$mwin->Button(
```

```
    -text => "Press me",
    -command => sub { $countmsg = $count++ . " presses"})->pack();
$mwin->Label(-textvariable => \$countmsg)->pack();
$mwin->Button(-text => "Quit", -command => sub { exit() })->pack();

MainLoop();
```

This program displays two buttons and two labels. The first label displays a rather redundant static text message. The text of the second label is set with -textvariable set to a reference to $countmsg. This variable keeps track of the number of times the first button is pressed. The first button does this with its -command parameter, which updates the $countmsg each time. Finally, there is a second button to quit the program. Here's what this one looks like after the button has been pressed a few times:

As with a Button widget, the background color of a Label can be set with -background.

Note that labels are widgets that can be placed anywhere in a window with pack(). One can also display a single line of text with the MainWindow title() method, which places a text message in the title bar of the window. Here is a little program showing both a title and a Label (along with a button to quit the program):

gui8.pl

```
use Tk;

$mw = MainWindow->new();
$mw->title("This is a title");
$mw->Label(-text => "This is only a label")->pack();
$mw->Button(-text => "Quit", -command => sub { exit() })->pack();

MainLoop();
```

Notice that the title() method does *not* create a widget, and therefore does not take the usual parameters. It takes only a single string argument defining the title, and does not need to be "packed". A Label, on the other hand, is a genuine widget, and therefore takes the usual parameters. Its own title is given by the -text parameter, and it must be placed with pack(). Here is how this program displays:

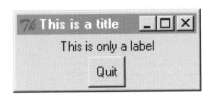

B.4.3   Radiobutton

Radiobuttons are a somewhat more complex widget. As with HTML radiobuttons, this widget provides for a set of mutually disjunctive choices. The user selects one by clicking on one of the set. In terms of Tk, a Radiobutton is similar to a Button; its text can be set with -text or -textvariable, it has a -command parameter, and its colors can be set with -background and -activebackground. However, in addition, it takes a -variable parameter and a -value parameter.

These latter two enable the distinct functionality of a Radiobutton. The -variable parameter takes a reference to a variable as a value. This variable both defines the set of Radiobuttons that are grouped together, and holds the value of the Radiobutton selected. The -value parameter takes some numerical or string value as an argument. If the relevant Radiobutton is selected, this value is assigned to the variable specified by -variable. Here is a simple example:

gui9.pl

```
use Tk;

$mw = MainWindow->new();
$mw->Label(-text => 'Make a selection')->pack();
$mw->Radiobutton(
    -text => 'German',
    -variable => \$lang,
    -value => 'g',
    -command => sub {
        if ($lang eq 'g') {
            $msg = "Sprechen Sie Deutsch?";
```

```
      } elsif ($lang eq 'f') {
          $msg = "Parlez vous français?";
      } else {
          $msg = "Do you speak English?";
      }
})->pack();
$mw->Radiobutton(
   -text => 'French',
   -variable => \$lang,
   -value => 'f',
   -command => sub {
     if ($lang eq 'g') {
         $msg = "Sprechen Sie Deutsch?";
      } elsif ($lang eq 'f') {
          $msg = "Parlez vous français?";
      } else {
          $msg = "Do you speak English?";
      }
})->pack();
$mw->Radiobutton(
   -text => 'English',
   -variable => \$lang,
   -value => 'e',
   -command => sub {
     if ($lang eq 'g') {
         $msg = "Sprechen Sie Deutsch?";
      } elsif ($lang eq 'f') {
          $msg = "Parlez vous français?";
      } else {
          $msg = "Do you speak English?";
      }
})->pack();

$mw->Label(-textvariable => \$msg)->pack();

MainLoop();
```

The program displays three Radiobuttons. Selecting one of the buttons sets the text of the subsequent Label accordingly. The program is long, but only because of repetition (which we address in the next program). The program begins in the usual fashion. What's new are the three Radiobuttons. Each one uses -text to display a different language name, and each one sets -variable to $lang, making them a mutually exclusive group of three. Each sets a different

-value as appropriate, and then each includes the same setting for -command. The value of $lang is used to set the $msg variable. That, in turn, is used to set the text of the last Label. Here's what the display looks like if we select "French":

Note that the program is exceedingly redundant; the same -command value is repeated three times. We can eliminate this repetition by setting -command to a reference to a named subroutine, and then putting all the repeated code in the subroutine. The following revision shows how this works:

gui10.pl

```
use Tk;

$mw = MainWindow->new();
$mw->Label(-text => 'Make a selection')->pack();
$mw->Radiobutton(
    -text => 'German',
    -variable => \$lang,
    -value => 'g',
    -command => sub { doLang() })->pack();
$mw->Radiobutton(
    -text => 'French',
    -variable => \$lang,
    -value => 'f',
    -command => sub { doLang() })->pack();
$mw->Radiobutton(
    -text => 'English',
    -variable => \$lang,
    -value => 'e',
    -command => sub { doLang() })->pack();
$mw->Label(-textvariable => \$msg)->pack();
```

```perl
MainLoop();

sub doLang {
    if ($lang eq 'g') {
        $msg = "Sprechen Sie Deutsch?";
    } elsif ($lang eq 'f') {
        $msg = "Parlez vous français?";
    } else {
        $msg = "Do you speak English?";
    }
}
```

Here the value of -command is a reference to a named subroutine: doLang(), which is given at the end of the program. The use of a named subroutine is possible with any widget with a -command parameter.

Named subroutines can also take arguments. Here's an example. This program does the same thing as the preceding one, but with Buttons, rather than Radiobuttons:

gui11.pl

```perl
use Tk;

$mw = MainWindow->new();
$mw->Label(-text => 'Make a selection')->pack();
$mw->Button(
    -text => 'German',
    -command => sub { doLang('g') })->pack();
$mw->Button(
    -text => 'French',
    -command => sub { doLang('f') })->pack();
$mw->Button(
    -text => 'English',
    -command => sub { doLang('e') })->pack();
$mw->Label(-textvariable => \$msg)->pack();

MainLoop();

sub doLang {
    $myLang = shift();
    if ($myLang eq 'g') {
        $msg = "Sprechen Sie Deutsch?";
    } elsif ($myLang eq 'f') {
```

```
    $msg = "Parlez vous français?";
  } else {
    $msg = "Do you speak English?";
  }
}
```

Here, the value for each button is stipulated in the subroutine call. Here's how the display looks when "German" has been selected:

B.4.4   Changing Things

One can manipulate the properties of widgets and how they are packed during the course of the program. This section introduces some of the simpler ways to do this.

To change a widget that has already been packed, one can use the configure() method. This method takes any appropriate parameter–value pair as an argument and makes the appropriate change on the designated widget. Here is a simple program that shows how this works. This program displays three buttons and a label. Selecting each different button determines the text and background color of the label:

gui12.pl

```
use Tk;

$color = 'red';
$text = 'This is red';

$mw = MainWindow->new();
$label = $mw->Label(-textvariable => \$text, -background => $color);
$label->pack(-side => 'bottom');
```

```
$b1 = $mw->Button(-text => 'red', -command => sub { doColor('red') });
$b1->pack(-side => 'left');
$b2 = $mw->Button(-text => 'yellow', -command => sub { doColor('yellow') });
$b2->pack(-side => 'left');
$b3 = $mw-> Button(-text => 'blue', -command => sub { doColor('blue') });
$b3->pack(-side => 'left');

MainLoop();

sub doColor {
    $color = shift();
    $text = "This is $color";
    $label->configure(-background => $color);
}
```

Since the text of the Label is set with -textvariable, we need only change the value of that variable to change the text. However, there is no analogous "variable" option with the -background parameter, so we use the configure() method to change the color. Here's what the display looks like:

We can also change which widgets are displayed and what order they are displayed in dynamically. The simplest way to remove a widget is with packForget(). This doesn't destroy it, but only stops displaying it. It can be redisplayed by invoking pack() again. Here is a simple example. This program displays a button that toggles the presence of a second button:

`gui13.pl`

```
use Tk;

$b1text = 'show';

$mw = MainWindow->new();
$b1 = $mw->Button(-textvariable => \$b1text, -command => sub { doit() });
$b1->pack();
$b2 = $mw->Button(-text => 'Quit', -command => sub { exit() });
```

```
MainLoop();

sub doit {
   if ($b1text eq 'show') {
      $b1text = 'hide';
      $b2->pack();
   } else {
      $b1text = 'show';
      $b2->packForget();
   }
}
```

The text of the first button is set with -textvariable, enabling it to shift between "show" and "hide". Notice how the first button is created and packed, but the second button is created and not packed. The program begins with only a single button displayed.

The first button invokes a subroutine unimaginatively called doit(), which either shows the button (by packing it), or hides the button (with packForget()). The text of the first button changes accordingly. Here is what the two displays look like:

 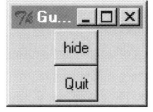

B.5   Graphic Experiments

In this section, we create yet another version of our syllable-counting experiment, this time making use of the Tk module. The experimental details are kept simple, so we can focus on the GUI aspects that Tk provides.

The general logic is as follows. We will be presenting our subjects with a list of items and soliciting their judgments about the number of syllables in each item. The experiment program will have three phases. First, the instructions for the experiment will be given. The subject presses a button to move to the next phase where the experimental items are presented. After giving their response to each of the items, there is a final phase where the subject is thanked.

In the first phase, we will need a large Label to hold the instructions, and a Button which will move the subject to the second phase. In the second phase, we will need a Label for the experimental items, and several Radiobuttons for subject responses. Finally, in the third phase, we will need a Label for the "thank you" message, and a Button to end the program. Moving between these different phases, and showing and hiding the different widgets needed will entail some careful higher-order logic. We go through the program step by step, showing how that logic works:

tkexp.pl

```
use Tk;

@items = ("hat", "flour", "charity", "cowl", "flower", "towel", "syllable");
$b1text = 'Continue';
$introflag = 0;
$instruc = <<"MYEND";
This is an experiment testing your ability to count
the number of syllables in a word. For each of the
following items, you should indicate how many syllables
it has by clicking the appropriate button. There are
seven items in total.
MYEND
$date = localtime();
print("\nnew subject: $date\n");
. . .
```

The first bit of the program above initializes the nongraphical elements of the program. The @items array holds the experimental items.[3] The $b1text variable is the -textvariable that the first button of the program uses. The $introflag variable will be used to keep track of what phase of the program we are in: 0 for the first phase, and 1 for the other two. The instructions displayed in the first phase of the program are assigned to $instruc using here-document syntax. Finally, each subject's results are preceded by a date stamp:[4]

```
. . .
$mw = MainWindow->new();
$mw->configure(-background => 'mistyrose');
$mw->title('Syllable-counting experiment');
$mw->Label(
    -text => 'Syllable-counting experiment',
    -background => 'mistyrose')->pack;
```

```
$b1 = $mw->Button(
   -textvariable => \$b1text,
   -command => sub { intro() })->pack(-side => 'bottom');
$ins = $mw->Label(
   -text => $instruc,
   -background => 'mistyrose')->pack(-side => 'bottom');

MainLoop();
. . .
```

This next batch of code initializes the GUI elements needed for the first phase of the program. These widgets call various subroutines which are responsible for moving the subject to subsequent phases and for recording the subject's responses. There is, as usual, a MainWindow. Just for esthetic appeal, we set the background color of relevant widgets to the color "mistyrose". We set the title of the window, and then position two labels and a button. The first label simply displays the title of the experiment again. The second label displays the instructions. The button invokes a subroutine intro(), which moves the subject to the next phase of the experiment. The text of this button will change over the experiment, and so it is given as a -textvariable:

```
. . .
sub intro {
   if ($introflag == 0) {
      $introflag = 1;
      $ins->packForget();
      $b1->packForget();
      $mw->Label(-textvariable => \$wordtext,
         -background => 'coral')->pack();
      $wordtext = shift(@items);
      $rb1 = $mw->Radiobutton(
         -text => "one",
         -value => 1,
         -variable => \$response,
         -background => 'mistyrose',
         -activebackground => 'OrangeRed',
         -command => sub { doResponse() })->pack();
      $rb2 = $mw->Radiobutton(
         -text => "two",
         -value => 2,
         -variable => \$response,
         -background => 'mistyrose',
         -activebackground => 'OrangeRed',
```

```
        -command => sub { doResponse() })->pack();
    $rb3 = $mw->Radiobutton(
        -text => "three",
        -value => 3,
        -variable => \$response,
        -background => 'mistyrose',
        -activebackground => 'OrangeRed',
        -command => sub { doResponse() })->pack();
  } else {
    exit();
  }
}
. . .
```

The intro() subroutine is a complex one. It is invoked in the first or the third phase of the experiment and its behavior is determined by the value of the $introflag variable. In the first phase of the experiment, the intro() method hides the button and instructions, displays the first item of the experiment, and sets up three radiobuttons. In the final phase of the experiment, this method simply quits the program:

```
. . .
sub doResponse {
    print("$wordtext: $response\n");
    if ($#items > -1) {
        $wordtext = shift(@items);
        $rb1->deselect();
        $rb2->deselect();
        $rb3->deselect();
    } else {
        $wordtext = 'Thank you!';
        $rb1->packForget();
        $rb2->packForget();
        $rb3->packForget();
        $b1text = 'Dismiss';
        $b1->pack(-side => 'bottom');
    }
}
```

Each of the radiobuttons calls the doResponse() subroutine, which also has two functions. If there are subsequent experimental items, it displays the next item, and deselects all the radiobuttons. If there are no more experimental items, it removes the three radiobuttons, brings back the button, and moves to the third phase of the experiment. The only thing new here is the deselect() method, which deselects the radiobuttons.

Here's what the first phase of the experiment looks like:

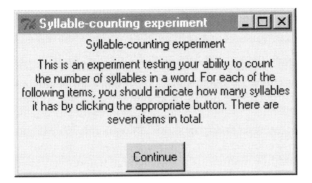

Here's the second phase:

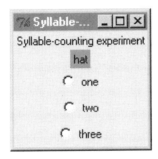

Here's the final phase:

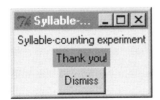

B.6   Summary

This appendix has introduced the very useful Tk module. While this is a powerful tool, it requires that you understand object-oriented programming and references. In addition, it can be difficult to install and is not available on all architectures.

This section has only scratched the surface of what can be done with the Tk module. There are a huge number of additional widgets and methods that have not been covered here.

Notes

[1] Under the hood, Tk is extremely complex. What it actually consists of is an entirely separate programming language glued onto Perl. Fortunately, you don't need to know anything at all about the Tk programming language to make use of the Perl Tk module.

[2] With the release of MacOS 10, Tk should be available for Macs.

[3] They should be randomized, but we leave this step out to focus on GUI details.

[4] The results should be written to a specific results file, but this detail is also left aside.

Appendix C
Special Variables

Here are some of the special variables that Perl provides. Many of them have an alternative mnemonic name that can be accessed if you include the declaration use English; at the beginning of the program. This list does *not* include many special variables that pertain to topics not treated in this book.

$_ ($ARG)   The default input and pattern-searching space.

$1, $2, $3, . . .   The patterns from the corresponding set of parentheses from the last pattern-match.

$& ($MATCH)   The string matched by the last successful pattern-match.

$` ($PREMATCH)   The string preceding whatever was matched by the last pattern-match.

$' ($POSTMATCH)   The string following whatever was matched last.

$+ ($LAST_PAREN_MATCH)   The last bracket matched by the last pattern.

@+ (@LAST_MATCH_END)   Holds the offsets of the last matches.

$/ ($INPUT_RECORD_SEPARATOR)   The input record separator.

$, ($OUTPUT_FIELD_SEPARATOR)   The output field separator.

$0 ($PROGRAM_NAME)   Contains the name of the program being executed.

$[The index of the first element in an array, and of the first character in a substring. Default is 0.

$]   The version of the Perl interpreter.

$^O ($OSNAME)   The name of the operating system.

$^T ($BASETIME)   The time the program began running.

$ARGV   The name of the current file when reading from <>.

@ARGV   Contains the command-line arguments.

@INC   Contains the list of places that require, or use look for their files.

@_   Within a subroutine, contains the parameters passed to that subroutine.

%INC   Contains entries for each filename included by do, require, or use.

%ENV   Contains the current environment.

$! ($ERRNO)   The value of the current error.

Appendix D
Where to Find Out More

We have really only scratched the surface of what there is to know about Perl in this book. There is a lot more to learn and lots of ways to find out more.

D.1 Documentation

The documentation that comes with Perl is extensive. The most useful tool is the perldoc command. With appropriate command-line flags and arguments, this can be used to find out much. First, to find out about the command itself, use perldoc perldoc. This will return all the ways the command can be used.

The most useful way to use the command is perldoc -f X, where X is some Perl command. For example, perldoc -f split will tell you how to use the split() command.

The perldoc command can also be used with a single argument without a flag. In this case, the argument is the name of one of the sections of the Perl manual, or the name of an installed module. The command perldoc perl gives a list of these sections. For example, perldoc perlref presents the section of the manual dealing with references.

Finally, another very useful function with perldoc is the -q flag, which searches for a keyword in the FAQ. For example, perldoc -q reference will return those questions in the FAQ dealing with references.[1]

D.2 The Web

There is a huge amount of information available about Perl on the internet. There are a number of interesting sites, some of which I list below. One that deserves special mention is www.cpan.org, the "Comprehensive Perl Archive

Network". This is where you can get *all* Perl modules. In addition, it is a repository for all sorts of useful Perl documentation.

http://www.cpan.org "Comprehensive Perl Archive Network", the repository for *all* modules and lots of other info.
http://learn.perl.org A site for people learning Perl.
http://www.perl.org "Perl mongers", a Perl advocacy group.
http://use.perl.org A Perl community news and discussion website.
http://www.perl.com A commercial site, but with lots of useful information.

D.3 *The usenet*

There are several usenet groups devoted to Perl. The most useful are the comp.lang.perl and comp.lang.perl.misc groups. However, these are not recommended for the beginner. Discussion in these groups is occasionally quite high level, but also occasionally rather silly. The web resources and documentation are far more useful as places to get started.

D.4 *Other Books*

There are several other books that are of use to the Perl/linguist programmer.
   Programming Perl by Larry Wall, Tom Christiansen, and Jon Orwant (Cambridge, Mass.: O'Reilly Press, 2000) is *the* definitive reference on Perl. It is an excellent compendium of information, but can be quite daunting to a newbie.
   Learning Perl by Randal L. Schwartz and Tom Phoenix (Cambridge, Mass.: O'Reilly Press, 2001) is an excellent *general* introduction to Perl.
   Programming for Linguists: *Java™ Technology for Language Researchers* by Michael Hammond (Oxford: Blackwell, 2002) is an introduction to programming in Java for linguists. This is a different programming language from Perl, but you may find that it fits your needs better for some applications. The advantage of the Java programming language is that it provides for much more elaborate GUIs. In addition, it allows for more elaborate web-based programming. On the other hand, it is necessarily object-oriented (for better or worse), and does not offer integrated regular expressions.

Note

[1] The ActiveState™ version of Perl for Windows also puts all of these documents into HTML so that you can view them in your web browser instead.

Index